"Move over, Lucy Ricardo; here comes Nancy Kennedy! I wish I could say I loved reading about Nancy's foible-prone life because it's so unlike my own, but the truth is I can relate far too well! The good news is that Nancy's insights into what it means to be an imperfect woman loved by a perfect God left me feeling encouraged and even grateful, although I'll probably never look at chicken salad the same way again."

—KAREN LINAMEN, author of *I'm Not Suffering from Insanity...I'm Enjoying Every Minute of It!*

"*When Perfect Isn't Enough* gave me hope that Proverbs 31 is not just a post-card from the spiritual, virtue-al heights, but a truth that authentic women can live out every day. Nancy's ability to combine rich, biblical insight with her everywoman antics provides a lift for the mind and spirit. (If only it could do the same for my *body*...)"

—ANITA RENFROE, comedienne and songwriter

"If you want a read that will make you laugh out loud—a read that actually describes your life in a way you've not yet confessed—then your next read should be *When Perfect Isn't Enough*. Nancy Kennedy may not be perfect, but now I can laugh and even rejoice in the fact that I'm not perfect either. You will love this book!"

—LINDA EVANS SHEPHERD, author, speaker, radio host, and founder of Right to the Heart of Women

"If you're tired of the condemnation, guilt, and obsessiveness that often accompany religion, you're going to love this book. I know it's for women and I'm a guy, but as I read this book, I'm reminded of God's love, his acceptance, his grace, and his laughter. Guys need that too. Nancy Kennedy is a major benediction!"

—STEVE BROWN, author and professor at Reformed Seminary in Orlando, Florida

When Perfect
Isn't Enough

Nancy Kennedy

When Perfect Isn't Enough

How I Conquered
My Fear of the
Proverbs 31
Woman

WATERBROOK
PRESS

WHEN PERFECT ISN'T ENOUGH
PUBLISHED BY WATERBROOK PRESS
2375 Telstar Drive, Suite 160
Colorado Springs, Colorado 80920
A division of Random House, Inc.

ISBN 1-57856-568-5

Library of Congress Cataloging-in-Publication Data
Kennedy, Nancy, 1954-
    When perfect isn't enough : how I conquered my fear of the Proverbs 31 woman / Nancy Kennedy.—1st ed.
    p. cm.
    ISBN 1-57856-568-5
    1. Bible O.T. Proverbs XXXI, 10-31—Meditations. 2. Kennedy, Nancy, 1954—Anecdotes. 3. Women—
Humor. I. Title.

BS1465.4.K46 2003
248.8'43'0207—dc21

                                                            2002154347

Printed in the United States of America
2003

10 9 8 7 6 5 4 3 2

This book is dedicated to Diane Cortese,
a woman who knows where to go to find virtue.

Contents

Contents

A Note to My Readers

In 1995 someone from a publishing company called and asked if I would like to write a book for them. At first I laughed.

"I don't know how to write a book!" I told the woman. Up to that moment, I had only written funny stories for magazines like *Christian Parenting Today* and *Marriage Partnership*. So they assigned me a talented editor, Shari MacDonald Strong, who helped me shape those stories into a book: *Help! I'm Being Intimidated by the Proverbs 31 Woman*.

Seven years and six books later, that first fearful plunge into the world of book publishing has been one of my most requested books. I'm pleased that WaterBrook Press is publishing it as *When Perfect Isn't Enough*, with the same stories as the original version, plus added devotional and study material.

I want to thank everyone who wrote and requested this book after it went out of print. That means a lot to me. God has been so gracious.

Now as you begin reading this book, my prayer is that you will hear God's voice assuring you that he loves you dearly, just as you are, and that in Christ you have already been made perfect.

Proverbs 31:10-31

A wife of noble character who can find?
She is worth far more than rubies.
Her husband has full confidence in her
and lacks nothing of value.
She brings him good, not harm,
all the days of her life.
She selects wool and flax and works with eager hands.
She is like the merchant ships,
bringing her food from afar.
She gets up while it is still dark;
she provides food for her family
and portions for her servant girls.
She considers a field and buys it;
out of her earnings she plants a vineyard.
She sets about her work vigorously;
her arms are strong for her tasks.
She sees that her trading is profitable,
and her lamp does not go out at night.
In her hand she holds the distaff
and grasps the spindle with her fingers.
She opens her arms to the poor
and extends her hands to the needy.

When it snows, she has no fear for her household;
for all of them are clothed in scarlet.
She makes coverings for her bed;
she is clothed in fine linen and purple.
Her husband is respected at the city gate,
where he takes his seat among the elders of the land.
She makes linen garments and sells them,
and supplies the merchants with sashes.
She is clothed with strength and dignity;
she can laugh at the days to come.
She speaks with wisdom,
and faithful instruction is on her tongue.
She watches over the affairs of her household
and does not eat the bread of idleness.
Her children arise and call her blessed;
her husband also, and he praises her:
"Many women do noble things,
but you surpass them all."
Charm is deceptive, and beauty is fleeting;
but a woman who fears the LORD is to be praised.
Give her the reward she has earned,
and let her works bring her praise at the city gate.

Introduction

Dear Mrs. Proverbs Thirty-One Woman,

I must confess, I never really thought much about you until recently. To be honest, I've always tried to avoid you. Please don't take this personally—I'm sure you're a lovely woman. I mean, your husband praises you, and your children rise up and call you blessed, and all (and next to my mom, you probably make the world's best apple pie).

What I want to know is, how do you do it? How do you get up early, bring food from afar, plant a vineyard, speak with wisdom, make coverings for your bed, build up your biceps, and do all the other stuff? Do you take vitamins plus iron plus calcium plus minerals? If not, then what's your secret?

Does your husband ever leave his orange peels wrapped up in a dish-towel so that when you pick it up the peels fly all over the floor? How do you find time for him at the end of a long day? Does he *always* consider you worth more than rubies?

Tell me, Mrs. P., are you content with your life? Do you have any regrets? Do you ever feel like changing your name and not telling anybody because you just…can't…do…another…thing?

Frankly, I find your list of daily activities rather intimidating. I wish I could do everything you do (with the exception of holding a distaff and grasping a spindle—mainly because I don't know what they are), but I don't see how I could possibly squeeze one more thing into my already busy schedule. When do you find time to consider a field and buy it? Before you extend your hand to the needy? After you watch over the affairs of your household? And what do you look for, anyway, when you consider a field for possible purchase?

What I really want to know is, how did you ever get your kids to rise up and call you blessed? Forget the blessed part—how do you get them to rise up? Do you unplug the television? Sew marbles in their back pockets? Tell them that couch potatoing is the leading cause of terminal acne?

As for their calling you blessed, either you have a front seat in the car for each of them, or they all have their own Playstation set. You probably remember your kids' names and would never embarrass them by wearing your bathrobe when you drive them to school or by drawing happy faces on your middle schooler's lunch bag.

Are you perfect? Are you the Superwoman everyone's made you out to be? Do you *always* speak with wisdom? Are you *always* noble and worthy of praise?

Or are you like me?

Do you ever accidentally-on-purpose forget to apologize to the woman you yelled at on the fifth-grade field trip because it's…well, it's just easier not to? Do you tell yourself one more Oreo won't hurt, then cry because you're too fat? Do you forbid one daughter from leg shaving until she's thirteen, then let the younger one do it at age eleven?

Do you think God will only accept you if you live up to some incredibly high standard instead of relying on grace and grace alone?

Mrs. P., perhaps I've been wrong about you. Maybe the secret to your life is not so much in the things you do but in who you are. Still, you've managed to accomplish some pretty impressive things, and that brings me back to my original questions. *How* do you do all that you do? More specifically, am I able to do it too?

We really should get together someday. Perhaps on a day when you're not out selecting wool and flax or trading profitably or supplying merchants with sashes. Maybe you could give me some tips on How to Be a Virtuous Woman in Three Easy Lessons. I'd appreciate any help you can give me.

Sincerely,

Nancy Kennedy

P.S. Do you happen to know how to get the washing machine to stop eating socks?

Chapter 1

Next on Oprah: The Virtuous Woman and Those of Us Who'd Like to Wring Her Perfect Little Neck

Who can find a virtuous woman?
PROVERBS 31:10, KJV

It was Mother's Day. No, maybe it was the time our church held a week-long women's seminar. Maybe it was just another ordinary Sunday. Whenever it was, my daughters were sitting next to me in the pew, writing on each other's shoes, while I sat in my usual Sunday worship posture, trying to untwist my pantyhose with one hand and cover a coffee stain on my white blouse with the other. I'd forgotten to brush my teeth that day too.

The pastor stood to speak.

"Open your Bibles to the book of Proverbs," he said. "Let's take a brief look at this beautiful passage of Scripture on womanhood."

His voice dripped with syrup. His eyes glazed over. He looked right at me.

My skirt button popped off and rolled out into the aisle. "I'm in trouble," I whispered to myself.

"Shh!" shushed the people around me.

Giving up on the pantyhose, I flipped through the pages to the passage listed in the bulletin, quickly scanned the text, and cringed, "Oh her…"

That Proverbs Thirty-One Woman. Her list of virtues reads like a personal ad: worth more than rubies, early riser, hard worker, et cetera, et cetera, blah-blah-blah.

I have a confession to make. Usually I love reading the personals. You know the ones I mean:

> Overworked college student on crutches, De Niro–
> Seinfeld combination. I'm an oyster in search of a
> pearl, Tarzan in search of a Jane, Howdy in search
> of a Doody. No chubbies or phony psychos.

Or:

> Midwest Mermaid, loves water and workouts, beaches
> and boating, swimming and sunsets. In search of tall,
> long-haired, caring, single, white male with good
> sense of humor, full set of teeth, and nice car. Must
> be REAL. No geeks or gutter beasts.

But the personal ad King Lemuel wrote when he went a-hunting for a queen always leaves me cold.

There's no way I can be like this woman, I thought as the pastor waxed eloquent on this paragon of virtue. *This is not life, this is not real!* I drove home from church in a decidedly unvirtuous funk and spent the rest of the day stewing and spewing and chopping onions.

By the time my husband came in from watering the lawn, I had viciously sliced, diced, and julienned nearly every vegetable in the house. As he walked into the kitchen, I stabbed the last tomato and turned on him. "Say, Barry," I asked as casually as I could, tomato guts splattered all down the front of me. "What's your idea of the perfect woman?"

"Why, uh, you, of course."

I wasn't convinced he was sincere. I suspected the knife poised in my hand may have influenced his answer just a tad.

Later, when the knife had been stashed safely inside the dishwasher and all sharp objects were out of my reach, I asked him again.

"Okay, say you weren't married to me; what kind of woman would you want to marry?"

"This is a trick question, isn't it?"

I could tell we were getting nowhere, so I opened my Bible and read him King Lemuel's personal ad:

> Wanted: One woman of impeccable character. Must be completely trustworthy and bring her husband good (not harm) all the days of her life. Must be an early riser, hard worker, great cook, and a shrewd businesswoman. Needs to make all her own clothes, as well as her family's. Must know her way around the real estate game and be generous to the poor. Oh, a green thumb and a tongue filled with wisdom and faithful instruction are required. In other words, she needs to "bring home the bacon, fry it up in a pan, and never let me forget I'm a man..."

When I'd finished, I asked Barry what he thought of her. Basically, he said what King Lemuel said. ("Who can find a virtuous woman?") Only Barry's version sounded more like, "That's some babe. Too bad they don't make 'em like that anymore."

"Get real," I answered. "I mean, he also expected her to meet merchant ships, spin her own thread, and plant a vineyard."

"Sounds good to me," he said, ducking the shoe I accidentally flung across the room.

Now I'm no Bible scholar, but this passage of Scripture seemed to scream at me that if King Lemuel were alive today, he would add to his list: the Virtuous Woman (we'll call her VW for short) is up to date on world events, has a body like Cindy Crawford's, and greets her family à la Donna Reed/Harriet Nelson/June Cleaver (pearls and high heels optional, milk and cookies required).

Today's VW wakes up (at 4 A.M.) spunky and chipper, ready to start the day with prayer time (in French) and an hour of step-aerobics before she reads the *Wall Street Journal* and writes her weekly newsletter to all her known relatives here and abroad.

She eats less than thirty grams of fat per day as recommended, can do a quadratic equation in her head, and never stashes packages of M&M's away in the cupboard or selfishly hoards them from her family, calling them "Mom's special vitamins."

Today's VW fixes okra and lima beans in such a way that her family clamors for more. She knows how to get mustard stains out of white silk, and she dusts regularly—even way up high where no one can see. Her saddlebags are on her horse, not on her hips.

Today's VW can hit those awkward notes in "Silent Night" and the "Star-Spangled Banner," fix her own flat tires, quilt while tutoring the neighbor's children in calculus (for free), and refuse telephone solicitors selling burial plots in a manner so effective that they don't ever call back.

She never misses a PTA meeting or open house at school, and she NEVER wrestles the television remote control away from her husband. Not only that, but whenever *The Good, the Bad and the Ugly* is on for the twelve jillionth time, she doesn't complain that she'd rather watch something else. She simply smiles and passes the popcorn (air-popped, lightly salted).

Where does all this leave me? Same place it leaves you—feeling like last week's moldy bread. I mean, the VW's children arise and call her blessed. Mine arise and tell me the milk's sour and they need exactly one hundred beans or popcorn seeds in a plastic Baggie RIGHT NOW before the bus (*honk! honk!*) comes. And while the VW is clothed with strength and dignity, I'm having a stellar day if my socks match and my shirt's buttoned correctly.

Later that evening, with the background music of a drippy kitchen faucet and the strains of two separate radios blasting two separate songs from two separate daughters' bedrooms, I sat slumped in my chair at the dining room table, my Bible open before me. Then dust from the dining room light fixture AND inspiration hit me at the same time. I arose, clutched my hand to my breast, and shouted, "As God is my witness, I will do it! Line by line, verse by verse, with all that is within me, I will become that Proverbs Thirty-One Woman. I can do it! I WILL do it."

Or die trying.

In that solemn moment of total surrender, I closed my Bible and brushed chandelier dust from my hair, trembling in fear at the journey that lay ahead of me. A tear trickled down my cheek and mingled with the dust on my face.

"Lord," I prayed, "if this is what you really want of me, if this is what my family needs, then Lord, *Thy will be done.*"

The Measure of My Worth

It's no secret: I want Meg Ryan's face and Cindy Crawford's body. I want Oprah's money and Julia Roberts's laugh.

Closer to real life, I'd like to be as funny and quick-witted as my friend Shelley, as articulate as my pastor, and as street-smart as my husband. Plus, I'd like to be able to drive someplace without getting lost.

Then throw in all my other unattainable goals like obeying the Ten

Commandments, cultivating the fruit of the Spirit, living up to the Sermon on the Mount, and I might as well give up and spend the rest of my life sitting on the couch watching reruns of *Murder, She Wrote.* I'll never be what I want to be. I'll never be what others want me to be either. I'll never measure up. I'll never be all I could or should be.

And that's the good news.

That's *the* good news, the gospel. In his Word, God sets before us a standard of perfection. He puts skin around it in the person of Jesus. He says, "This is my beloved Son, in whom I am well pleased" (Matthew 3:17, KJV).

Then he gently lets me know I'll never meet his standard no matter how hard I try; I'll never be perfect on my own. However, through the grace of God, when I turn to him in faith, Jesus' glorious perfection is credited to me.

In my Father's eyes, I already have the perfection of Christ. That means I can stop striving for a goal of flawlessness that I'll never be able to grasp and instead rest secure in the confidence that I am worth far more than rubies. I am accepted, cherished, and treasured beyond my wildest imagination—even without Meg Ryan's face and Cindy Crawford's body.

Digging Deeper

1. Who in today's society is held up as the "perfect woman"? What is your idea of perfection? How would your life be different if you were perfect?

2. Although perfection is an unreachable goal outside of our relationship with Christ, excellence is still a worthwhile pursuit. Different Bible translations describe the woman of Proverbs 31 as "a good wife" (RSV), "a virtuous woman" (KJV), "a wife of noble character" (NIV), and "an excellent wife" (NASB). Read 1 Corinthians 12:31–13:13 and Titus 3:1-8. What qualities are associated with excellence? How do they apply to your life? How are they attained? (See Titus 3:5.)

3. Scripture passages such as Proverbs 31, 1 Corinthians 13 (the "love chapter"), the Sermon on the Mount, the Ten Commandments, and all the laws found in the Old Testament are intimidating, to say the least. No one can do all that God requires! In light of that, why was the Law given to us? Take a look at Romans 3:19-28 and 7:7, then write out what you learn about the purpose of the Law.

4. Read Romans 3:23-24; 10:9-10; Ephesians 2:8-9; and Galatians 2:19-21. To the best of your understanding, what does it mean to be saved or to have faith in Christ? If Christ's righteousness or perfection is ours and we no longer need to strive for our own perfection, what should be our goal? Here are a few scriptures to get you started: Romans 7:6; 1 Corinthians 10:31; Galatians 5:6; Ephesians 1:17-19; 3:16-19; 4:15-16; Philippians 1:9-11 and 3:13-14.

"Do you find yourself caught in a performance trap, where no matter what you do it doesn't seem to be enough? Is a standard of perfection driving you further and further into despair and depression? Please listen carefully: That's not God's standard or expectation; it's someone else's. God doesn't enslave his sons and daughters; he frees them and enables them to serve.

"Don't keep trying to measure up to a standard that's not his. If need be, get some outside help, but take serious steps to cut the shackles holding you down. Oh, what a relief it will be!"

—STEVE BROWN, *Jumping Hurdles, Hitting Glitches, Overcoming Setbacks*

Chapter 2

Metal Head:
My Life As a Tin Man

Her husband has full confidence in her.

PROVERBS 31:11

I woke up the next morning still trembling from the vows I had made the night before. Or maybe it was because Barry had thrown the covers on the floor and our bedroom was a chilling sixty-five degrees.

I jumped out of bed and looked out the window. Everything looked the same, but *I* was different. I was about to embark on a quest for True Virtue. Proverbial Perfection. VW-hood. I opened my Bible to review my first assignment: getting my husband's full confidence.

"Piece of cake," I said. "I can knock this one off in no time." Slamming my Bible shut, I ran out into the kitchen to share the good news with my unsuspecting man.

"Barry," I said a few minutes later as I buttered toast just the way he likes it (getting every inch of the bread, not missing a spot), "I know in the past I've done a few things that might be interpreted as, well, as a teeny bit flaky, but I want you to know, you can have full confidence in me from now on."

"How so?" he asked.

"Well, I've been thinking. Remember the time I washed your wallet with your fifty-dollar hockey tickets inside, and you couldn't take your friends to the game, and you got all mad at me for not checking your jeans pockets?"

"Game four of the semifinals, three rows up from center ice—how could I forget?"

"And remember the time you told me to get flat latex paint for the dining room walls, and I accidentally got oil-based gloss enamel and came home and painted the walls myself to surprise you? And remember how I forgot to cover the heirloom hutch your Aunt Gertie left you, and it got all splattered with paint that wouldn't come off, and we had to get that antiques guy to completely redo the whole thing, and it cost almost two weeks' pay?"

"Of course I remember—we're still paying for it. What's your point?"

I placed the toast in front of him and then, after he'd taken the first bite, snatched the rest away when I noticed a huge moldy spot on the crust.

"My point is, I'm not going to do stuff like that anymore. See, I'm starting already, saving your life."

Barry ran over to the kitchen sink, full of newfound confidence in me, and spit out the moldy toast. He turned back around to face me. "I don't want to hurt your feelings, and I know you mean well, but…"

He didn't have to finish. That "but…" said it all, and he was right. I'm a creative, impulsive, do-it-first-then-read-the-directions kind of person. I'm the one you want at your party, but not the one you want to design your house—I might forget to put in closets. Barry, on the other hand, was doubly blessed with common sense. Don't think for a moment I'm not thankful for that.

Just then, the guy from the sheet-metal shop called to tell Barry that the heating duct piece he needed was ready. He asked if the piece could be picked up right away.

"Let me do it!" I mouthed to Barry. "I'll do it, I'll do it. I can do it!"

He took a breath and ran his hand through his hair. "Okay, Dan," he said. "I'll send my wife over today."

Bingo. Full confidence. Piece of cake.

Barry wrote down the directions to Dan's shop and handed them to me. "This is important," he said. "It's called a Y, and it's the only one left in the county. Remember, today's the day before Thanksgiving, and I need it for Friday. Just pick it up and bring it home. That's all you have to do. Got it?"

"Got it."

And that's exactly what I did. As soon as the girls went off to school, I drove out to Dan's, picked that baby up, and went right home. Full confidence. Piece of cake.

I didn't count on being bored.

Now I'm not bored very often, but when I am, I tend to get...*creative.*

I looked over at the piece of sheet metal sitting on the kitchen table and tried to decide how it would look as a hat. It was shaped sort of like a bottomless watering can, with an opening at the bottom just big enough for my head.

I put it on and danced around the room a bit, pretending I was the Tin Man from *The Wizard of Oz* and singing, "We're off to see the wizard."

That got boring, so I shoved the thing down over my face so only my eyes peeked through the "spout." This time I sang, "I'm a little teapot, short and stout."

When that became boring and I went to pull my "hat" off, I suddenly found that I wasn't bored anymore—I was stuck. Stuck with a piece of sheet metal on my head that caught underneath my nose and smashed my lips. Stuck. As in, "I'm in big trouble."

I yanked and pulled until I thought my nose would come off, which, you'd realize if you'd ever seen my nose, isn't such a bad idea. However, I didn't have time for do-it-yourself rhinoplasty. I had to get that thing off my head before Barry got home.

From my perspective, I didn't have many options. If I cried, I'd rust. (I remembered that from *The Wizard of Oz.*) If I waited until Barry got home, I'd end up somewhere over the rainbow.

I reached for my Bible with the faint hope that this had once happened to the VW and I'd missed it. Fortunately, I kept a bookmark right at Proverbs 31 and found it right away. Unfortunately, as I read down the text (no small feat considering my viewing area had only a six-inch radius and I had to hold the page over my head and lean backward), I didn't find anything about the wearing of metal chapeaux.

My eyes did land on "She does not eat the bread of idleness." Technically, I wasn't working on the B of I verse, but I took the opportunity to rejoice. When (if) I got out of my predicament, I could write off two verses! Yes, I realize I may have been a bit on the idle side; however, I wasn't eating bread. I know it's a stretch, but when you have sheet metal stuck on your head, your reasoning also gets stuck—or at least compressed—and doesn't function properly. My rejoicing was short-lived, however. As hard as I tried, no amount of yanking would get that baby off.

"All right, Lord," I prayed, "I promise—I really, really, really promise—I'll never do it again if you get me out of this thing."

Then I waited for my metal headpiece to miraculously break free. The longer I waited, the more I panicked. Finally, when I realized a miracle wasn't in my immediate future, I dialed 911.

"Mffrrffffth," I said. Actually, I said, "Help! I have a piece of sheet metal stuck on my head, and if I don't get it off, my husband will ship me off to Kansas—and my little dog, too!" but it came out as, "Mffrrffffth."

Maybe it sounded like I had a gag in my mouth and my arms and legs were all taped up, or maybe it sounded like I was trapped inside a piece of sheet metal. Whatever the case, the paramedics came within minutes.

They yanked and tugged (and laughed, I might add) as I clicked the heels of my ruby red sneakers saying, "Get me out of this thing! Get me out of this thing!"

After what seemed like years, they gave up tugging and brought in the Jaws of Life. Okay, so it was a pair of tin snips, but the result was the same. Through the little opening where just my eyes showed, I watched the paramedic named Jeff snip his way down the spout, coming dangerously close to my nose.

Click, click, click went my heels. The closer he came, the faster I clicked. As if he'd done this before, he stopped right where air ended and my nose began. Next, he snipped up past my chin and back to the air-nose spot. Finally he peeled it off of me.

Ah, I was home, Toto.

Free at last, free at last. Thank God Almighty, I was free at last. And as soon as the paramedics left, I got on the phone and called every sheet metal shop within a fifty-mile radius. The Full Confidence thing, you know.

I found one of those Y-thingies forty-nine miles away, rushed there, used my own "someday I want a new bedspread" money, and made it home in time to meet the school bus, start dinner, and peel sweet potatoes for the next day's Thanksgiving meal.

But before you think we all lived happily ever after with my family none the wiser, I have to tell you about my lips. Being smashed by sheet metal made them puffy, sort of like Sylvester Stallone's lips when he got the daylights beaten out of him by Carl Weathers in *Rocky.* I smeared them with lipstick and told my daughters I was going for the collagen-injected look that's popular with all the high-fashion models. They didn't buy it.

Neither did Barry.

When he came in, he took one look at me, turned to the sheet metal sitting on the table, and then stared back at me—smeared with lipstick and clicking my heels.

We got through dinner, got through the entire evening for that matter, without saying a word about my foray into the land of Full Confidence. At the end of the ten o'clock news, I turned to Barry, who was sitting on the couch next to me.

"Want a good-night kiss?" I asked.

He reached over and pulled a mangled hunk of metal out from behind the couch and put it between us. "How'd you get a fat lip?" he asked.

I blabbed the whole story to him and waited for flying monkeys to swoop down and take me away.

Instead, he just laughed. And then he laughed some more. When he got done, he laughed again. Finally he kissed my forehead (the lips grossed him out) and turned off the television.

"Barry, does this mean you have full confidence in me after all?"

"Shoot, no," he answered. "But I am impressed that you went to all that trouble to correct your mistake, using your own money and all."

I smiled a puffy smile. "What will it take to gain your full confidence?"

"A lifetime probably," he said. "But you could start by not sticking your nose—or in this case your whole head—where it doesn't belong."

"I can do that. But what else?"

He paused and thought for a moment. "You know. The little things. Mailing the electric bill instead of letting it sit on your desk. Putting my tools back in the toolbox after you use them. Stuff like that."

And then it hit me. Those things show my husband that I respect and love him. Such simple things, yet so doable—and so important to Barry. Still, I wasn't satisfied. As we walked down the hall on our way to bed, I asked him, "If I do all that, then will I have your *full* confidence?"

He looked at my fat lips and laughed. "Tell you what. You get me a pair of hockey tickets, three rows up from center ice, and we'll talk."

A Woman Worthy of Trust

Have you ever played the Trust Me game? That's where you're paired with a partner, with one of you as the "faller" and the other as the "catcher." The faller allows herself to drop backward, completely, totally, fully trusting that the catcher won't let her crash to the floor.

That level of trust should characterize any healthy relationship. Those around us should be able to trust us to be true to our commitments, honest in our conversation, and honorable in our conduct.

Such trust is especially important in marriage. In his book *What Men Want*, H. Norman Wright lists ten intimacy needs in marriage, with number one being security, which involves trust. He writes, "You can depend on the one you trust.... You can count on that person to back you and to praise you, not only in your presence, but also when you are not there."

Here's a secret about men: They deeply fear being considered inadequate, especially by their wives. They desperately want to be thought of as capable, strong. In the workplace they're constantly struggling to prove their adequacy. So when a man has one person whom he can trust to be on his side, to keep his secrets, to meet his needs, and to be his "catcher," he finds security. When he's secure, he's free from at least one of his fears, and he's grateful.

Oh, to be such a woman for my man! But how?

The first step is fully trusting that God is my Catcher. When I'm convinced that God is on my side, that he loves me completely, I'm secure. *I'm grateful;* I want to please God with my life.

He then takes that desire and fashions me into, among other things, a woman worthy of trust.

Digging Deeper

1. Think of someone you trust. What character traits make this person trustworthy?

2. Using a dictionary and/or a thesaurus, look up the words *trustworthy* and *faithful.* List all the nuances of these two words. Then using a concordance, look up the verses where these two words appear. From your findings, how would you describe a faithful, trustworthy woman? List the areas of your life in which you would like to demonstrate faithfulness. Ask God to make you into a woman worthy of trust.

3. According to the following verses, what does the Bible say about faithfulness: Psalms 85:10; 86:15; Proverbs 3:3; 14:22; 16:6; 20:28; Galatians 5:22-23? To what is it closely tied?

4. We love because God first loved us (1 John 4:10). Choose a passage of Scripture, such as Psalms 103; 105; or 106, that recounts God's faithful acts of love. Write out a prayer of praise to the Lord extolling his faithfulness in your life.

～

"You can fall in love, but you can't fall in trust. Trust doesn't come from romantic dinners and kisses on the doorstep. Trust, unlike love, is not blind. Trust is based on time, experience, and year-in, year-out faithfulness. It takes a few turns of the calendar before [a woman's] husband has full confidence in her."

—LIZ CURTIS HIGGS, *Only Angels Can Wing It*

Chapter 3

The Do-Him-Good Agenda

She brings him good, not harm,
all the days of her life.
PROVERBS 31:12

Let me set the record straight. I didn't mean to do it—any of it. You have to believe me; it was all an accident. I was just trying to, you know, do my husband good, not harm, all the days of my life. Besides, all's well that ends well, right?

It all started as my friends and I were sitting around my kitchen table, talking. As always, the subject of husbands came up. We started with the usual, "My husband *never* (blah-blah-blah)." "Well, at least yours (yakety-yak)." "*Mine* (yada-yada-yada)." You know the routine. After a while, someone changed the subject and began with, "Wouldn't it be fun to do like the books and magazines say and go off on a surprise weekend?" You know, the whole romance bit. Then the excuses started rolling.

Carol went first. "You know I'd do it, but we're still papering the hall bathroom."

Stephanie shrugged her shoulders and pointed to the baby attached to her breast. "I'm still nursing Max and can't leave him yet."

Poor Judy didn't have to say a thing. The last time she and her husband, Don, went away, she had twins nine months later.

All eyes turned to me. I gulped. My mission, should I choose to accept it: Plan a weekend away with Barry.

"No prob," I said. "I can handle it."

A week or so later I packed up the car with a picnic dinner, dropped the girls off at Grandma's, and in my best madcap, Julia Roberts way, surprised Barry at work, announcing that I was whisking him away for the weekend.

"I don't want to whisk," he said.

"Nonsense," I argued. "We haven't whisked in a long time. Besides, it'll Do You Good."

After a brief discussion (which I won), we whisked off into the sunset. Shortly before six o'clock, we arrived at our first destination: a deserted beach cove where we ate the chicken salad sandwiches I'd packed in my picnic basket that morning. Almost immediately we discovered why the cove was deserted: The wind seemed to come blasting out of nowhere (actually, it was from the east), whipping sand and bugs into our ears and our eyes and our sandwiches.

One of us wanted to leave, but the other one called him a wimp and insisted that we stay. (I had to. The Do-Him-Good agenda and all.)

Finally, when one of us couldn't take it any longer, he stumbled up the sand dunes, picking bugs out of his teeth, and hid out in the car, listening to the ball game on the radio. I followed, not too sure he wouldn't drive off without me.

After rinsing my sandy teeth with Diet Pepsi and dumping sand out of my shoes, I slid into the passenger seat and flipped off the radio. "Okay, time to turn off the ball game."

"But, but, but…," he said.

We rode along in ball-gameless silence while I waited for witty repartee. I waited a long time.

Finally Barry cleared his throat as if to speak. My heart fluttered at the hope of a meaningful tête-à-tête. Then, "Why do you have to do that with your teeth?" he asked.

"Do what?"

"That. You always make that clicking noise. Like you're chewing air." He demonstrated.

"I don't do that!" I answered, then pointed my finger at him. "At least I don't eat Styrofoam cups. You can't drink a simple cup of coffee without eating the cup. Most people throw theirs away, you know."

We chewed and clicked for a mile or so until we came to a winding, bumpy road that tossed us at every turn. This wasn't part of the Do-Him-Good agenda—and neither were the waves of nausea and the sharp pains that took our breath away as we were overtaken by an unmistakable bout of black death and/or food poisoning.

Green-faced, Barry steered the car into the parking lot of the first motel he saw and leaned his head on the steering wheel.

"We can't stay here," I said. "This is one of those motels that charge by the hour."

His face changed from green to gray and back to green again. "Do you want to die out here instead?"

A long-haired guy who I thought I recognized from *America's Most Wanted* stopped beside our car, belched, and scratched his armpit. Then he flashed a five-toothed grin at me.

That's when I decided, no, I didn't want to die there. We dragged our turning-greener-by-the-minute bodies into the office, signed the register, paid for the next twelve hours, and crawled off to Room 132 to... Well, if you've ever had food poisoning, you know what came next. I'll spare you the details.

Sometime during the middle of the night, we died. At least we thought we did. We each saw a bright light, but it turned out to be the red, blinking, neon sign that said MOT L.

As the room spun, we noticed it had been decorated in Early Sleaze motif. You know, clown-hair orange shag carpeting, an avocado green and harvest gold floral bedspread, black velvet paintings of bullfighters hanging cockeyed on peeling, green-and-black flocked wallpapered walls.

I reached over, turned on the cracked amber glass lamp chained to the dresser, then died again for a few hours as I rolled together with my snoring husband in the center of the sagging mattress, his elbow in my ribs.

Occasionally we were partially revived by the sounds of doors opening and closing, heavy footsteps parading up and down the hallway, and a pay phone ringing about every fifteen minutes. Resurrection came at 7:00 A.M. when a man calling himself Big Buck pounded on the door demanding to see Marie. At 7:01 Buck picked the lock and kicked the door open.

Weak and trembling, we called out from under the covers, "No Marie in here!" Fortunately, Big Buck left as quickly as he came. After he did, we shoved the dresser against the door, showered, put on our same clothes (don't you hate it when you forget something?), and dragged ourselves back to the deserted beach cove to sleep the day away.

Hours later we awoke, sunburned, mosquito bitten, and scratching, but alive and feeling relatively chipper. One of us announced he was ready to call it quits, but the other one again hinted at someone being a wimp. "Where's your sense of adventure?" I demanded.

"I think I lost it somewhere back at the motel, along with the chicken salad."

I checked my Do-Him-Good agenda. "Barry, you'll love what comes next: a room overlooking the Atlantic Ocean."

He scratched at the raised, red bumps all down his leg. "I don't want to go," he said.

"It'll Do You Good."

"So will an enema, but I don't want one."

I pulled out my big guns. "It's paid for and nonrefundable."

"Let's go."

When we arrived at the door of our beachfront inn, I asked Barry to wait outside while I ran in. Taking a bag of silver confetti out of my purse, I sprinkled it on the bed and around the room. Then I set little candles all around the wooden ledge surrounding the bed, lit them to create a romantic glow, and beckoned Barry inside.

Yeah, we smelled. Yeah, we had gunky teeth and bad breath, not to mention sand in our hair and day-old clothes on our bodies. Despite all that, we succumbed to the glow of the flames, although not quite the way that was called for in my Do-Him-Good agenda.

As we kissed, getting silver confetti in our hair and embedded in our skin, I began to feel warm…no, hot…all over.

"We're on fire!" I gasped. We had knocked a candle over and set the blanket ablaze.

We flew off the bed. As Barry beat the flames with a pillow, I helped by screaming and pouring a can of soda all over the sheets, the carpet, the bedspread, and everything else. Never before had two lovers produced such sparks!

We spent the rest of the evening laughing as we scrubbed soda stains out of the rug, ate takeout Chinese food, and watched reruns on Nick at Nite—all the while estimating how much we owed in damages.

"Barry," I said, snuggling up to him as he started to nod off, "you know I only want to do you good, not harm."

"I know," he answered, "and you do, when you're not poisoning me or setting me on fire."

"Really?"

"Really."

I decided to leave it at that, mainly because he began to snore. I, on the other hand, couldn't sleep. Food poisoning and embedded confetti aside, I couldn't help thinking about ways I'd done Barry real harm: not-so-subtle admiring looks at other men; caustic, careless words; demands to have things my own way.

I thought back to when Barry was unemployed and wanted to look for work out of state, but I adamantly demanded we stay in southern California—I didn't want to move away from my family. He continued to seek work there, but at that time jobs were nonexistent. My unwillingness to adjust my priorities caused him harm as he wrestled with the need to provide for his family and the desire to please and appease me.

But then I remembered ways I had done him good. Finally saying good-bye to my family and moving away with him. Standing by him at his father's funeral. Telling him I love him and believe in him, even during times he can't believe in himself. Praying daily that he will come to know the love of God. Telling him in all sincerity, "Barry, I think you're a wonderful provider, and I appreciate the ways you sacrifice for me and our two daughters by putting us before yourself. I'm proud of you."

Eventually I, too, drifted off to a peaceful, nonnauseous sleep. As I did, my last thought was of the next day's Do-Him-Good plan: Cancel Do-Him-Good bungee jumping; listen to ball game on the way home.

What Makes a Good Wife?

About thirty years ago a book called *The Total Woman* spelled out what it meant to be a good wife. Such a wife was much like the woman of Proverbs 31, only *more so:* She met her husband at the front door wearing nothing but plastic cling wrap and a smile.

Being a newlywed as well as a new Christian, I wanted to be a good wife, so I tried the clear plastic bit. It failed to produce the desired reaction of eternal devotion, servitude, and adoration from my husband. All I got was a hearty chuckle. My husband thought I was joking. He didn't understand that I was desperately trying to be a Good Wife. At that time, I read any book I could get my hands on, searching for quick-fix ideas, lists of dos and don'ts, easy steps, proven principles.

Just tell me what to do!

I didn't realize then that goodness is not what we do but a result of who we are. Or, more accurately, *whose* we are. Goodness is a fruit of God's Spirit, who dwells in every believer in Christ.

Do you want to be a good wife? Judith Lechman writes in the *Women's Devotional Bible,* "We soon find it all but impossible to live the Christian life with our own strength and goodness. It is through God's strength that we know courage, and through his power that we know goodness. When we realize this, surrender becomes our priority."

As we surrender to the goodness of God, he produces that same fruit in us. We have his goodness, and with that, we can be good wives—plastic-wrapped or not.

Digging Deeper

1. A good cup of coffee, a good book, good gas mileage for your car. We use the same word to describe so many things. What makes something good? What do you think makes a woman a "good" wife?

2. Read Psalm 107. Make a list of all the ways God showed his goodness to his people. How has God shown his goodness to you?

3. Read Luke 6:27-45. What are some of the qualities of "goodness" described in this passage? (Note: This passage does not advocate suffering abuse. If you are being abused, please seek help.)

4. Goodness always shows itself through action. The Proverbs Thirty-One Woman did "him good, not harm, all the days of her life." What are some ways wives harm their husbands? If you're married, what are some ways you can do your husband good? Read 1 Peter 3:1-6. Regarding the subject of "doing him good," what does the scripture say to wives of unbelieving husbands? What are some practical ways Christian wives can "do good" to their non-Christian husbands?

~

*"We read, 'She does him good and not evil / All the days of her life.'
Note that this commitment was... for all the days of her life. Such a
statement indicated a decision of her will (not an emotion) to stand
by his side forever, regardless of what happened to them. Today it
seems common to love your husband and do him good until problems
come."*

—LINDA DILLOW, *Creative Counterpart*

Chapter 4

Liddle Lambzy Divy

She selects wool and flax and
works with eager hands.

PROVERBS 31:13

In her hand she holds the distaff
and grasps the spindle with her fingers.

PROVERBS 31:19

One night an acquaintance, Kathy, called. "I heard from a reliable source that you've gone off on some sort of a spiritual adventure. Do tell. How's it going?" she asked.

I heaved a soulful sigh. "Oh, you know. I tried to do Barry good, not harm, but instead I made him sick." I gave Kathy all the gory details.

"Hmm. You know I'm only saying this as a friend and because I really care about you, but don't you think you've done enough? I mean, you've already driven your poor husband to his knees. You don't want to kill the man, do you?"

"No. I just want to be like *her*."

"Her who?"

"The Virtuous Woman—VW—from Proverbs 31."

"Oh, *her*. Personally, I think she's just a figment of some Old Testament ad exec's imagination."

"No, you're wrong, Kathy! The VW was real and alive, and I'm going to be just like her. You'll see."

"And what verse are you trying to conquer today?" Kathy scoffed into the phone.

I grabbed my Bible and opened it to the dog-eared, tear-stained page. "She selects wool and flax and works with eager hands."

"Pshhh! And just how are you going to do that?"

I thought for a moment. "Well, I don't know exactly. Do you have any suggestions?"

"You could go into sheep ranching."

I laughed at the thought of herding a flock of sheep around my neighborhood. Still…it wasn't that bad of an idea. Lots of people who lived near us raised goats and horses and pigs. A sheep or two might work. Besides, that just might be another two-for-one opportunity. With a sheep of my own, I could select wool, use my eager little hands to work, and even spin my own thread with a spindle or two. Bingo! Verses 13 and 19 accomplished in one shot.

"Hello! Hello! Are you there?"

Kathy's voice jolted me out of my thoughts. "I'm sorry, Kathy, what were you saying?"

"I said, I'll be praying for you, sweetie. Ta ta."

"Yeah, ta ta." I set down the phone and held my head in my hands. I still liked the sheep idea, which isn't surprising, because I'm a real sucker for animals. I can't pass up a box of free kittens or a pathetic whimper from a dog at the pound. As a result, we now have a big Labrador retriever and seven or so cats running around our little house. Understandably, Barry has given me strict orders not to bring home one more stray. And so I sighed and decided I'd have to find another way to measure up to the standard set in this verse.

Now the day in question just happened to be the day before Barry's birthday. I'd been saving money all year for a recliner for him. He'd always wanted one of those buttery-soft, all-leather, superdeluxe, megacomfortable, "chair of kings" type recliners. At the furniture stores they cost roughly the same as a new car, but at the flea market out at the fairgrounds, a man named Bud sold them for $250. (The catch being, you have to pick them up yourself.)

So I got up bright and early the next morning prepared to do just that. However, to accomplish my mission, I needed to borrow Barry's truck— no small task. You see, I'd never driven it before, and to all of a sudden request it might raise suspicion. To pull off my surprise successfully, I needed a keen mind and a quick wit. Or at least a good lie.

"Barry," I said as he stirred his morning coffee, "I need to use your truck today. The school principal has asked all parents with trucks to help with the annual hayride."

"That's funny," he said. "I never heard anything about a hayride."

"Well, that's because this is the first annual one, and they just decided on it last night. Yeah, and they called while you were in the shower just a few minutes ago."

He didn't answer at first. He just shot me one of those "I'm not buying this" looks, like when I tell him dust on furniture really does help protect the wood. He handed over the keys anyway. What a guy.

After he left for work in my car and the girls had left on the school bus, I climbed into the pickup he affectionately calls "Little White" and took off for the flea market at the county fairgrounds.

I have to tell you, I love flea markets, especially this one. They sell everything from canned pole beans to battery-powered wipers for eyeglasses, from snakeskin belts to custom bathtubs. Bud and his recliners are there every Wednesday, right next to the livestock pens.

That's how I met Shirley.

Shirley had white curly hair, shining brown eyes, and a bleat so pitiful it would make you cry.

"What's wrong with that sheep?" I asked the livestock lady.

"Honey, sometimes they jist know when they's fixin' to become lamb chops," she said with what I considered evil relish. "I got a guy comin' anytime now to take this one to the butcher shop." She made a cut-throat motion and laughed. "He'll be eatin' good tonight."

I looked over at Bud, who was dusting off the chair I had picked out for Barry. Then I looked over at Shirley. (At least that's what I named her. She might've been a Stanley for all I knew.) Shirley looked back at me and bleated for help.

Suddenly all the legs of lamb and lamb chops I'd eaten through the years took on names: Beverly Shank Stew, Louis Chop, Sylvia with mint jelly and new potatoes. I couldn't let Shirley end up as some guy's main course.

"How much for that sheep?" I asked the livestock lady.

"I told you. I already got a guy fixin' to buy her."

"How much is he paying?" I asked.

"Two hundred cash."

"I'll take her for $250." And with that, I handed over my chair money. Bud didn't look pleased, to say the least. Avoiding his disgruntled squint, I trotted Shirley down the center aisle of the flea market and into the parking lot.

Then it dawned on me. What do you do with a three-hundred-pound sheep? I hadn't thought about it until we got to the truck. She was too big to fit in the cab and too heavy to hoist into the back. I lowered the tailgate and tried shooing her in. She wouldn't shoo. I grabbed a handful of popcorn and threw it in, hoping she'd hop in after it. She didn't hop.

After much coaxing, pulling, pushing, wheedling, and a little bleating (on both our parts), I finally convinced Shirley to walk up a board I leaned against the tailgate.

I think she sensed I was a friend. Either that or she was tired of being shoved around, because once she got inside the truck, she plopped down and went to sleep. The whole ride home I entertained myself with thoughts of hand-sheared, hand-knitted wool sweaters.

Not only that, I knew Shirley would be a welcome addition to our home (Barry's initial shock notwithstanding), both as a pet and a source of my family's warmth. Dare I say it? I felt *virtuous,* as in the Proverbs Thirty-One VW kind of virtue. My eager fingers twitched at the prospect of carding my own wool. Never mind that I didn't know how to knit, let alone shear and card and whatever else must be done to wool before it becomes a sweater. (Not to mention that the closest I'd ever come to taking care of a sheep was pouring Worcestershire sauce on chops before putting them in the broiler.)

When we got home, Shirley got down from the truck a lot more easily than she had climbed in. That gravity thing. I must say, she immediately took a liking to our yard; she ate a huge patch of ivy by the front fence and nibbled the lavender crapes right off our crape myrtle tree.

"Stay," I ordered her and went around the side yard to open the garage door.

It seems sheep don't *comprende* simple commands. Honest, I only turned my back for a minute, but Shirley managed to wander into our neighbor George's yard and use his horseshoe pit for a litter box, knocking over a section of our split-rail fence in the process. As big and fat as she was, that sheep could move.

By the time I got over the fence, Shirley had pulled half of George's laundry off the clothesline and was heading right for his carefully sculpted topiary bushes (or in sheep terms, "lunch").

It was about then that I started having second thoughts about bringing Shirley home. Chairs don't usually eat your neighbor's landscaping or knock over fences. On the other hand, chairs can't provide your family with wool either. It's one of those Catch-22 situations.

What would the VW do? I wondered. Obviously, she'd go with the sheep, since they didn't have *Jeopardy* on TV back then and, therefore, no need for reclining chairs.

As mentally stimulating as this whole situation was (and no doubt I could've gone on for hours debating the merits of chairs vs. sheep), a sudden thunderstorm put an end to my musings. Shirley, obviously *not* a fan of Florida's sometimes-violent weather, went berserk. She started running all over the yard, knocking over rosebushes and the picnic table and tearing up the lawn.

What could I do? I had to get her inside somewhere, and the only somewhere available was the garage. Except we don't really have a garage. Last year we converted it into a combination laundry/storage room. Actually, Shirley might've been fine there until the storm passed, but when Barry and I took down the door that leads from the garage into the house, we never got around to putting it back on. (You don't think about sheep when you're remodeling.)

I chased Shirley around the yard, calling, "Here, sheepy, sheepy! Here, Shirley!" She didn't listen. Or if she did, she ignored me. I can't say that I blame her. I had to physically tackle her, tie a rope around her neck, and drag her—and I mean, D-R-A-G her—into the house.

Now, I'm not a complete idiot. I dried her off with a towel and even wiped off her muddy hooves. Then I set up a barricade of kitchen chairs and an old tool chest so she wouldn't come into the kitchen.

How was I supposed to know sheep can climb?

Since I thought she'd curl up and go to sleep in front of the dryer like my cats do when they come in from a storm, I went off to take a shower and change my clothes—until a loud noise startled me.

Somehow Shirley had made her way into the living room. By the time I found her, she'd chewed up half a magazine and part of a candle and was heading for one of Barry's work boots. *This is not good,* I thought.

I weighed my options: live with a furry bulldozer who runs amok on autopilot, risking the loss of my home and possibly my marriage, or return Shirley and sentence her to certain death.

I decided I needed to have a heart-to-heart talk with my bleating friend. "Let's chat," I said and sat down next to her on the floor. "Listen, we've got a problem here. This isn't going to work. You've got to go, and I've got to find Virtue."

Not exactly the conversationalist I'd anticipated, Shirley merely baaed. While she did, I had this nagging feeling that I was somehow missing the point. As I sat there snipping bits of wool off her back and practiced pulling at it and twirling it into yarn, it hit me that the whole point of the verse I wanted to fulfill wasn't that she selected wool and flax and herded sheep around all day but that she worked with eager hands. And since she couldn't run off to Wal-Mart whenever she needed a spool of thread or a skein of yarn, she had to rely on spinning her own.

"Shirley," I said, scratching the top of her head, "I do lots of things with my hands." To prove it, I counted off on my fingers: "I sew, write letters to family and friends, braid my daughters' hair, pull weeds…" I kept on counting until I ran out of fingers—and I still had more to add!

Not only that, I realized I *like* working with my hands, and whenever I ask God to put them to work, he always finds something for them to do. All he asks is that whatever I do, I work at it with all my heart, as if I'm working for him and not for men. All I ask of him is that he direct my hands, because to be honest, without his guidance, they have a tendency toward evil.

As I sat there with my sheepish friend, I knew this was one of those times I needed God to guide my hands. They ended up dialing Andy's Petting Zoo in the next county. Andy came right over with his sheep truck, lured Shirley with sheep food, and took her away to frolic with other sheep. With eager hands, I waved good-bye and went inside to repair the damages.

By the time everyone got home, I'd scrubbed all the sheep tracks off the carpeting, propped up the fallen fence sections, and chatted with George about the unusual plant-munching, laundry-stealing storm we'd experienced earlier.

For Barry's birthday I bought him a power drill and fixed his favorite meal—leg of lamb—only, I substituted chicken for the lamb. I think he noticed, even though he said he smelled lamb from all the way down the street.

The best part of the whole adventure is I discovered I don't have to do anything extraordinary to be like the VW in this verse. No, the best part is, I saved Shirley's life.

No, the *best* part is…no one ever caught wind of my experiment in sheep ranching.

How to Be "Handy"

Anytime my daughter Laura brings home a new friend, she always says, "Mom, show us your hands." She's fascinated by my abnormally small hands with their stiff, crooked fingers—each with only one knuckle. My thumbs, which are slightly out of place, don't bend at all. At least they provide cheap entertainment for my kid.

The Bible has much to say about hands: clean hands, holy hands, lazy hands, idle hands, diligent hands. The woman of Proverbs 31 had "eager" hands. She had zeal to serve God with her hands. In verse 20, the proverb says she "extends her hands to the needy." Her hands were an extension of a heart secure in the love of God.

Too often women serve with eager hands out of a sense of duty or obligation, out of a compulsion borne of insecurity and a need to draw worth from pleasing others. But God delights in hands that serve out of gratitude, as a pure response of love.

"Do not let your hands hang limp," writes the prophet Zephaniah. "The LORD your God is with you, he is mighty to save. He will take great delight in you, he will quiet you with his love, he will rejoice over you with singing" (Zephaniah 3:16-17).

When you think of God singing to you, you can't help but offer him your eager hands.

Digging Deeper

1. Think about the past twenty-four hours. Name everything you can remember doing with your hands. If you were to categorize them, which activities were done with eager or diligent hands and which with lazy or idle—possibly reluctant—hands?
2. Let's look at some of the different types of hands in the Bible.
    a. Clean. Read Psalms 18:20-24; 24:3-6; James 4:7-10. How do we get clean hands, and what reward will they bring?
    b. Holy hands, lifted hands. Read 1 Timothy 2:8; Psalms 28:2; 134:2; Lamentations 3:40-42. What prompts a believer to lift her hands to God?
    c. Lazy, idle hands. Read Proverbs 6:10-11; 10:4a; 14:1; 21:25; Ecclesiastes 10:18; 11:6. What warnings do we find in these passages?
    d. Diligent, eager hands. Read Proverbs 12:24; 10:4b; Ephesians 4:28; 1 Thessalonians 4:11-12. What are the benefits of working with eager hands?
3. What types of things can you do today with your hands, and how can you perform your work with all your heart "as to the Lord" (Colossians 3:23, KJV)?
4. Now let's study God's hands. Did you know your name is engraved on the palms of his hands (Isaiah 49:16)? Using a concordance or even an online Web site such as Bible Gateway (www.bible.gospelcom.net), do a search for the word *hands,* making note of each reference to God's hands. Select a passage

to memorize that will serve to remind you that God's hands are ultimately responsible for anything your hands accomplish. Here are a few suggestions: Deuteronomy 3:24; Psalms 17:7; 19:1; 37:23-24.

—

"Expect great things from God; attempt great things for God."

—WILLIAM CAREY, quoted in *God's Little Instruction Book for Women*

Chapter 5

How Much Afarther, Mom?

She is like the merchant ships,
bringing her food from afar.
PROVERBS 31:14

*C*all it a craving. Call it a yen, a hankering, an unbridled yearning if you will. Whatever you call it, I had it.

I wanted grasshopper pie.

Again.

As I sat, pondering the next verse in my Journey Toward Virtue, I crunched on a low-sodium gherkin (pickles being, according to one women's magazine, a surefire cure for a sweet tooth) and contemplated the lengths to which I'd previously gone to bring food home: driving twenty-five miles across town for Dairy Queen's Peanut Buster Parfaits, traveling the turnpike (and paying $5.25 in tolls) just for Godiva chocolates, bargaining with neighbors to bring me genuine Long Island potato knishes on their return from a trip to New York.

Then there was the time ten years ago when I drove two hundred miles round trip for grasshopper pie.

I'd had a hankering that day too. I also had a cranky toddler and a whiny seven-year-old who demanded to know why she couldn't wear her plastic "jellies" (shoes) to school and why she couldn't be an only child. Despite my threats to make her sister one, her whining continued—and so did my craving for grasshopper pie.

Common sense said, "Turn on *Sesame Street*," or even, "Put Laura down for a nap, and spend some Quality Time with Alison." However, at that moment, common sense was overpowered by the thought of minty green pie—one hundred miles away up the coast of California.

I really don't know what made me think of grasshopper pie. The truth is, I'd eaten it only once before, when I was a child and my Aunt Gladys ordered it for the two of us at a restaurant. I remember staring wide-eyed as she took a bite—fully expecting to hear the crunching of grasshopper bones. To my surprise, it turned out to be nothing more than mint pudding.

It is said four things are never satisfied: the grave, the barren womb, land without water, and a blazing fire. I'd like to add a fifth: a woman craving a minty, chocolaty dessert.

The powerful yearning left me no other choice but to pack up the kids and make the trek to the same restaurant where Aunt Gladys first introduced me to this wondrous creation.

Actually, the ride was rather pleasant. The girls occupied themselves quietly, singing songs, playing pat-a-cake, and generally behaving like perfect angels. No, wait a minute—that was a family I'd seen on TV. Our trip went more like this: Laura squirmed in her car seat, making grunting noises as she struggled to escape, while Alison continued to whine about her plastic shoes and moan about having to take a car trip on a day off from school.

Yeah, that's my family.

Anyway, not three miles out of town, the kicking began—fwump, fwump, fwump on the back of my seat.

"Laura," I said sweetly, "Mommy's back doesn't like to be kicked."

Squirm, squirm, kick, kick, kick.

"Laura," I repeated (a bit less sweetly), "Mommy says don't do that."

After we'd gone through this ritual three times, I pulled the car over and whipped around to hold her feet. "Laura," I said with absolutely no sweetness in my voice, "we're on our way for a nice drive to get some yummy pie. If you kick Mommy, she'll get a headache, and she won't be able to enjoy it. Now stop."

I turned back around in my seat, and as I started once again down the road—my mind set on pie—I felt a slight tap on the back of my seat. Tap (pause), then tap, tap, kick, kick, kick.

"I told you we shoulda got a dog instead of a baby," Alison said as I pulled the car over for the second time.

"You're not helping," I replied and got out of the car, this time with a better idea. I moved Laura's car seat to the other side—positioning it behind Alison—and set off again, with Laura still kicking and Alison still whining.

We'd only gone another couple hundred feet when I realized my plan wasn't working, so I pulled over again. This time I put Alison in the back-seat with Laura (amid protests of "I don't wanna sit with her!"), handed them each a can of apple juice and a handful of graham crackers, then hit the road again. This time we made it twelve whole miles.

"Potty!" called a voice from the backseat.

I pulled off the road AGAIN and drove to the nearest gas station.

"No big potty! Potty chair!" hollered Laura as I tried to coax her up on the rest room toilet.

"For Mommy?" I asked.

"Potty chair!" she yelled.

I pulled out my secret weapon. "For french fries?"

"Fuh-fries!" she cried and climbed right up. That salt and lard gets 'em every time.

After we all got situated (and I'd driven five miles out of the way look-ing for golden arches), I got back on the freeway and realized I had ninety miles yet to go.

For the next half-hour or so, all was quiet. Alison dozed off, while Laura rhythmically kicked the back of the front seat.

Then Laura smiled.

The only time Laura ever smiled in her car seat was after she had just thrown up. This time was no exception.

"Oh, yuck!" Alison yelled upon waking up from her nap. As she covered her mouth and gagged (and Laura continued smiling), I pulled over to clean up the mess.

I know I should have called it quits right there, but as I wiped off the girls, the car seat, the backseat, the floor, the windows…something in me snapped. It was no longer a mere food craving that spurred me onward but a drive to conquer all of life's obstacles.

With renewed determination, I veered off course for a brief trip to JCPenney's for clean clothes (plus spares), then settled back on course to go the distance, win my race, and obtain the prize.

The rest of the trip proved uneventful. Alison stared out the window counting red cars, Laura continued her rhythmic kicking, and I daydreamed about the creamy mint and crunchy chocolate reward awaiting me.

We arrived at the restaurant long after the lunch-hour crowd, and the hostess seated us immediately in a spacious booth. The waiter, attentive and prompt, took our order, patted each of the girls on the head, then returned with our just desserts.

Rarely does an event match the anticipation, but to my delight, this proved to be one of those times. The pie was every bit as delicious as I'd remembered, and I got just as big a kick out of introducing my own seven-year-old to the pleasures of eating odd-sounding delicacies as my aunt had with me.

We came, we saw, we ate green mint pie. We smeared green goo on the table, and with the exception of a spilled glass of soda, I deemed my mission a success. Like the apostle Paul, we had been hard pressed on every side, yet not crushed; struck down, yet not destroyed.

Plus, we experienced the added benefit of getting a piece of pie.

After we'd finished eating, I purchased a pie to take home as spoils of the battle and gathered up the girls for our journey homeward.

The Bible says the Virtuous Woman of Proverbs Thirty-One traveled afar to bring food home to her family. In today's world, with supermarkets and restaurants in every town, we don't have the same need to travel to far-off places. Even so, we wives and mothers follow in the footsteps of the VW when we see that our fridges are stocked and meals prepared (whether we're Galloping Gourmets or Canned Chili Queens in the kitchen).

Not only that, we feed our families in other ways. Whenever you show your child what the Bible says about "Who made bugs?" or horoscopes or how to deal with an enemy at school, you're feeding your family.

As for bringing food from afar, isn't it fun every once in a while to pack up the family and chase after a hankering?

I crunched another pickle and smiled as I recalled my long-ago fulfillment of the proverb's directive of "bringing food from afar." *I was virtuous back then, and I didn't even know it,* I thought as I marked the verse off my list.

However, that still didn't relieve my craving for grasshopper pie—and neither did the pickle. I popped the last bite into my mouth, picked up my car keys, and declared, "If I leave now for California, maybe I can be back by fall."

How "Afar" Will You Go?

In my "real life," I'm a newspaper reporter. Part of my job involves interviewing and writing the faith testimonies of people in my community for the weekly religion page. Many times I've had the opportunity to write about missionaries, and I've discovered they all have two things in common: (1) a passion for the gospel and (2) an overwhelming, burning desire to take it to the ends of the earth.

I remember one woman in particular who said she pined nearly her whole life to go somewhere far away as a missionary. However, she kept having babies. So for close to thirty years she raised a brood of little ones, all the while yearning to go to the mission field.

Just recently, at age sixty-eight, this woman has finally begun taking short-term mission trips to places such as Haiti and Albania, feeding the hungry and serving as a nurse in medical clinics. She says her missionary heart is finally at rest, but she now realizes that all the years she couldn't travel were not in vain. She spent those years "feeding" the Word of God to her own children with the same missionary zeal she felt for people of other nations. After all, a woman's family is her greatest mission field.

Because the woman of Proverbs 31 was a woman of virtue, she went to great lengths to see that her family had enough to eat, for their bodies as well as their souls. May the Lord create in us a heart to feed our families as she did.

Digging Deeper

1. Think of your favorite food. How far have you gone, or what have you gone through, to sample some of it? Can you say you have the same zeal when it comes to feeding your children spiritual truth?

2. In what ways can mothers (and grandmothers and aunts) influence children for Jesus? Briefly list the instructions or examples found in the following scriptures: Deuteronomy 6:5-9; Judges 13:8; 1 Samuel 1:10-11,20-28; Mark 10:13-16; Ephesians 3:14-19; 2 Timothy 1:5; 3 John 4. Pray and ask God to show you creative and specific ways you can apply these scriptures to your family.

3. Regarding the care and feeding of teenagers: It's not uncommon for teens to take a detour in their walk with God, even those raised in healthy Christian homes. Perhaps a child has never made a personal commitment to Christ. Or he or she did at an early age but now has wandered far from that commitment. The

good news is, a child can never stray outside the Father's grasp. Read Isaiah 30:20-21; 54:13; Ezekiel 36:24-27; Matthew 5:6. When your teen turns a deaf ear to your attempts to feed him or her God's Word, how can these scriptures encourage you as you pray?

4. Have you ever considered that unless we feed our own souls, we have nothing to feed anyone else? That's why it's vital that we incorporate Bible reading and study into our own daily diets. When you're seeking ways to satisfy your hunger, consider the words of the psalmist: "I have not departed from your laws, for you yourself have taught me. How sweet are your words to my taste, sweeter than honey to my mouth!" (Psalm 119:102-103). How have you been fed by the Word of God? Write out the scriptures that are especially meaningful to you and refer to them often. You may want to incorporate the scriptures in a prayer. If you're doing this study in a group, take turns sharing a passage of Scripture that's meaningful to you.

❧

"Communicating the priority of knowing God and following in his ways is the most important thing we can do for [our children]. And when this priority becomes their hearts' desire, then they will be after his heart."

—MYRNA ALEXANDER, *Women's Devotional Bible*

Chapter 6

Things That Go *Thump, Thump, Thump* in the Night

She gets up while it is still dark.

PROVERBS 31:15

Her lamp does not go out at night.

PROVERBS 31:18

There are some things that I really hate doing. I hate vacuuming out my car. I hate buying shoes and flossing popcorn skins out from between my teeth. And unlike Madam Proverbs, I especially hate getting up early.

Most of all though, I hate it when my husband's out of town and I have to stay alone. That's when the wimp factor kicks in full force.

Here's my routine: At the first sign of darkness, I go around and check all the window locks. Twice. I look under every bed and behind every door. Then with extreme caution lest Psycho-slasher Norman Bates should be in town, I check the showers. Next I put a pair of Barry's work boots out on the front porch and turn on all the outside lights. I then bolt and lock all the doors. If my two daughters aren't home, I put chairs under the door knobs and set out booby traps like roller skates and marbles under windows—sort of like Kevin did in *Home Alone.*

Also, if the girls aren't home, or later on when they're sound asleep, I might talk loudly, as if I'm with someone big and strong and mean. ("No kidding, you killed a mountain lion with your bare hands?")

If the girls *are* home, then I do without the marbles and skates (I don't want to frighten the girls) and make do with extra prayers. Of course, that works best, although burglars falling on marbles does make more noise.

The final step of my anti-Bogeyman procedure is to program 911 on my speed dial and put the Beware of Attack Dog sign in the window. Then I go to bed.

I know you're probably saying, "Woman, where is your faith?" Good question. In fact, that's the part of my routine I forgot to tell you about. Somewhere between checking the showers and putting out the boots, I have a conversation with myself that goes like this:

Me: "Woman, where is your faith?"

Me again: "I don't know."

First Me: "Doesn't God protect you whether Barry's here or not? Does he not watch over you? Does he not care? Is he not almighty and powerful?"

Me again: "Well...um... What was the question again?"

I never learn, you know. Take the last time Barry went out of town. The kids and I did the usual routine of dinner, dishes, packing school lunches, etc. When it came time for everyone to go to bed, I casually went through my routine and settled myself in for the night. ("Settling myself in" consists of propping pillows under the covers to make it look like a six-foot-tall body is asleep next to me. I've often considered using a melon as a pseudo-head, but I've never been able to find one that isn't shaped like...well, like a melon. Besides, sometimes they're not in season, and grapefruits just aren't menacing enough.)

Where was I? Oh yeah. After I settled in for the night, I turned on the TV. At that hour there's not much I'll watch. The news is out—too scary.

Same goes for *America's Most Wanted, Unsolved Mysteries, Cops,* or anything with *death, terror,* or *murder* in the title. That usually leaves *The Tonight Show* or reruns of *Green Acres* or *My Mother the Car.*

Usually I choose *The Tonight Show* and fall asleep halfway through Leno's monologue, or at least by the first Ginsu knife commercial. That night was definitely a Ginsu night.

I think it was during the part where the guy slices a can or a shoe that I finally managed to go to sleep. I'd been listening to the familiar night sounds of the Florida woods outside my window: frogs croaking, my cats walking on the window ledge, raccoons nibbling the leftover cat food, an errant armadillo tearing up our lawn.

Then IT happened. IT went *thump, thump, thump.* ITs thumping sounded unmistakably like the boots of a mummy-werewolf-vampire. IT sounded like IT wore a hockey goalie's face mask and had knives for fingernails and liked to attack green-eyed, knock-kneed, short women in pink pajamas. In other words, me.

Thump, thump, thump. IT sounded evil. Sinister. Definitely Bogeymannish. I strained to listen, my heart thumping almost as loudly as IT.

Thump, thump, thump.

My mind raced—what should I do? I knew what Lucy Ricardo would do. She'd signal for Ethel Mertz, and together they'd get into mischief. By the final commercial, they'd discover that IT wasn't a mummy-werewolf-vampire at all, but a bird caught in a chimney, a practical joke designed to teach them a lesson, or something equally as innocent—and with a laugh track.

This type of thing happened to the Brady Bunch too. IT usually turned out to be pranks played on the Brady girls by the Brady boys (also with a laugh track).

I, however, didn't have a laugh track or a script. I didn't even have a weapon.

"It's nothing, it's nothing, it's nothing," I repeated to myself.

Thump, thump, thump.

But it was something, it was something, it was something, because nothing doesn't thump. Something thumps.

I went down my mental checklist: Doors locked? Check. Got 911 on speed dial? Check. Boots out? Check.

I listened again, just to make sure it wasn't my imagination.

Thump, thump, thump.

Nope, imaginations don't thump. Hairy, carnivorous, beastly animals thump. Bogey-Animals thump.

My life flashed before my eyes. I grabbed a pen, and just as I was about to scribble out a will, I thought about seventeen-year-old Alison, just starting her senior year in high school, and little Laura, a brand-new middle schooler, both of them asleep down the hall.

I knew what I had to do.

"No Bogey-Werewolf-Freddy Krueger's getting my children without a fight!" I cried. Swiping my hairbrush off the dresser, I tiptoed out into the dark hallway to meet my fate.

I stood still—*thump, thump, thump.* I walked, no *thump.* I stopped again, *thump,* etc. The thump and I played this game for about five minutes as I went around checking everything. It wasn't the water heater or air conditioner, not a ceiling fan or even a drippy faucet. It was just a *thump.*

Then I saw IT through the living room window. Actually I saw ITs shadow—make that *shadows.* IT was two of IT. And IT was humanlike and holding something round and headlike. It appeared to be a basketball. *Only why,* I reasoned, *would a couple of vampires/ax murderers be carrying a basketball around at 1:37 A.M.?*

Then the ITs saw me. I just knew it. They held still; I held stiller. After about a jillion hours, the ITs—the Bogeymen, which looked a lot like the two boys who live down the street—boogied away, taking their thumping head with them.

The story doesn't end here, however. As I stood in the darkness, I thought about the Proverbs Thirty-One Woman and how she got up while it was still dark. Of course, her husband probably wasn't at a baseball card show in Fort Lauderdale overnight, and she probably didn't get up to chase away a *thump*. But that wasn't the point. The point was, I was up and couldn't go back to sleep, not knowing if the Thumper might return.

Then I had an idea. Actually I had an aha.

"Aha!" I said. "Since I'm up already, this counts as virtuously getting up early!" Although an insistent, nagging voice inside my head told me it doesn't count unless I go to bed, sleep, then get up while it's still dark. I simply dismissed those thoughts as fiery darts from the devil, who was surely trying to keep me from my quest. Instead, I focused on the part of the proverb that said, "Her lamp does not go out at night."

"Get thee behind me, Satan!" I cried. "Neither rain nor snow nor thumps in the night will keep me from performing my sacred duty. I MUST. I WILL." With a grimace of determination, I set out to spend the rest of the night—with all the lamps, overhead lights, TVs, and all major as well as minor appliances on—pursuing Virtue.

I scrubbed the crud from the pan underneath the refrigerator, baked three dozen brownies, solved an Unsolved Mystery, composed a sonnet in iambic pentameter, wrote my congressman, and got hooked on phonics. I polished the silver, clipped my toenails, and mated previously unmated socks. I ordered a nacho pan, a Galloping Gourmet V-Slicer, and two sets of Brick Royale T-Fal cookware from one of the home shopping channels. By the time the girls got up, hot corn muffins and fresh-squeezed orange juice sat waiting for them on the table, their outfits for the day had been ironed, and their homework was typed in triplicate.

Actually when you think about it, women—mothers in particular— spend much of their time caring for their families while the rest of the world sleeps. What mom hasn't sat up with a sick or scared child, nursed and rocked a baby, changed sheets or cleaned up vomit in the middle of the night? What about getting up at 4 A.M. to bake brownies for a school party because Mom hadn't been informed until the night before that it was her turn to provide snacks? What about time spent in prayer (or more often, in worry) when her teen is out late with the car?

By 8:00 A.M., with the girls out the door, I rested at the kitchen table with my virtuous yet tired head on my arms. I had spent the wee hours of the thumpless night caring for my family. I'd succeeded. I'd attained. I'd zzzzz. . .

At 8:03 I fell asleep, face first, in a plate of leftover waffles and syrup, and for the next few hours, I slept the sweet (yet sticky) sleep of an almost Virtuous Woman.

It's Time to...

God's ways are upside down. The last are first; those who lose their lives find them; and the busier our lives, the more necessary it is to be still before God.

I know that in my head, and I know that in my heart. But when I'm rushing around, a slave to my to-do list, it's nearly impossible to slow down, let alone stop. I feel guilty if I do...but I feel guiltier if I don't.

Martin Luther once said, "I have so much to do today that I shall spend the first three hours in prayer." Of course, he didn't have a dog to take to the vet, library books to return, a daughter who needs folders with pockets AND prongs, or seventy-five e-mails to reply to—all before noon. Luther could fit three hours of praying into his morning—twenty-four hours lasted longer back then—but in the past six centuries our days have grown increasingly shorter. Or so it seems.

Some days I hit the floor running at 5:30 A.M. and rarely get everything done by 10 P.M. With so much to do and the shortened-day phenomenon, even with instant coffee made in a microwave, three minutes is often hard to squeeze out of a morning. As it is, I find myself skipping meals, opting instead for Krispy Kreme doughnuts and coffee for breakfast and whatever's ninety-nine cents at Wendy's for lunch.

I don't mean to, but sometimes I skip God too. *No time today,* I tell myself. *Too much to do.* But when there isn't time for God, it's because time *is* my god and my to-do list is my master.

But when I turn it all upside down and take Luther's advice for busyness, resting in the presence of the Father, my to-do list becomes less of a tyrant, and the hours of my day grow to be more than sufficient.

Suddenly I realize that, with so much to do, I can't afford not to spend time on my knees.

Digging Deeper

1. Think about yesterday. How did you spend most of your time? How much time do you devote to work, rest, and recreation in an average day? Read Psalm 90:12 and Ephesians 5:15-20. What do these verses say about the use of our time?

2. In Genesis 1 and 2, God created the entire universe in one week. Included in that week was a day of rest, which he blessed and made holy. Read Deuteronomy 25:17-19; 2 Chronicles 14:6-7; and Isaiah 30:15. What do you learn about rest and why it is important?

3. Review Proverbs 31:10-31. Keep in mind that the woman in this passage couldn't have done all this in one twenty-four-hour day. Realistically, how would this woman spend her days in the twenty-first century?

4. Someone once said, "We master our minutes, or we become slaves to them; we use time, or time uses us." Think back over the past few weeks; how have you been a slave to your minutes? Pray and ask God to teach you to number your days and to show you what to change in your schedule.

—

"Every moment counts, not in the sense that we have to be constantly busy in order to prove our worth or make a mark in the world, but in the sense that all time is material that God uses to love us, guide us, correct us, redeem us."

—EUGENE PETERSON, *Praying with the Psalms*

Chapter 7

Burnt and Other Offerings
from My Kitchen

She provides food for her family.

PROVERBS 31:15

My Aunt Gladys always says, "Anyone who can read a recipe can cook," but I don't know if that's true. I can read. And I've certainly read my share of cookbooks. However, they don't tell you the really important stuff. For example, when the pumpkin bread recipe says, "Fill pans three-quarters full," it should also say, "If you fill them with more, the batter will rise up, plop over the side of the pan, fall on the oven's heating element, cause a pumpkin fire—and your husband will not be amused."

Likewise, when the recipe for baked pork chops says, "Bake at 350 degrees for forty-five minutes," it should continue, "but if you have to make an emergency trip to the store, DON'T increase the oven temperature to 500 degrees in order to decrease the baking time. Your pork chops will look and taste like shoe leather, your kids will use them as Frisbees, and once again your husband will not be amused."

That's not to say my cooking hasn't amused my husband at times. In between the food poisoning from chicken salad and regular visits from the fire department, he's found occasion to chuckle. He still laughs about the time I mixed up the package of orange Jell-O with the powdered cheese from the macaroni box and came out with macarongi and cheddarello.

The kids, on the other hand, don't know any better. They've grown up with the "if you put enough ranch dressing on it, you can't taste the burnt part" doctrine and the "black is beautiful/mushy is magnificent/lumpy is luscious" creed. Besides, if you add enough catsup, anything tastes good.

As I sat on the floor one day, leafing through the pages of *Remedial Recipes, Kooking with Konfidence,* and *101 Ways to Fool Your Family into Thinking Spam Is Really Meat,* it occurred to me that Scripture didn't say the VW provided gourmet, delicious, or even edible food for her family. It just said she provided food.

"I do that now!" I shouted. "Cheerios count! Toaster waffles qualify! Technically, canned spaghetti sauce on toast is considered food!"

I ran to cross verse 15 off my list—just in time too.

Laura walked in and dropped a bombshell that sent shock waves of doubt throughout my kitchen. Earlier that week I'd made the mistake of letting her eat at a friend's house. Ever since, she'd seemed troubled about something. That day I found out why.

As I stirred a pot of macaroni on the stove, she announced that I wasn't like other moms. "You don't make REAL food. You know, stuff like pot roast and meat loaf. Mashed potatoes. Peanut butter cookies and biscuits."

To that, Alison, who'd come walking in behind her, added, "Yeah, Mom. I mean, how many ways do you think you can keep disguising boxed macaroni and cheese? Even Dad can tell."

I gave the macaroni another stir and sat the kids down at the table. Just moments ago I'd made peace with myself concerning my virtuous provision of food for my family. However, I knew I had to explain a few things to my children. The time had come for them to learn the truth. And because truth is often more easily digested through a story, once I'd mopped up the macaroni that had bubbled and overflowed all over the stove and pried stuck pasta off the bottom of the pot, I sat down to tell them this one:

"Once upon a time, a beautiful, multitalented woman desired to be a gourmet cook. Or at least one that didn't send dinner guests to the hospital with ptomaine poisoning. She bought herself a Crockpot, which came with a recipe for split-pea soup. But even though she followed the recipe exactly, after eight hours the peas were still hard and her impatient husband was hungry.

"So, she had an idea: 'If I pour the HOT peas into the blender, put the top on and turn it on full blast, maybe it'll mush into soup.'

"However, the beautiful woman didn't know that the heat from the peas would make everything expand. To her surprise, the top shot off the blender, and pea soup flew all over the cupboards and the ceiling, the counters, the floor, the walls—everything.

"And then it hardened.

"Her insensitive husband laughed at her and then went to Burger King while the beautiful woman stayed behind to scrape their dinner off with knives and pancake turners. (She was not only beautiful but tidy, too.)

"The next day she decided to bake a pie. Her first pie. A few months after they were married, the woman's husband mentioned that his mom made the world's best peach pie. Now the husband didn't realize it at the time, but what he really said was, 'My mom is perfect and I don't think you can measure up.' He also didn't realize that the beautiful woman would take his comment as a challenge. Unfortunately, the beautiful woman couldn't figure out how to use a rolling pin, so she brought home a frozen peach pie instead."

I stopped my story just long enough to open the windows and fan the smoke from my burning macaroni out of the kitchen. After dumping the burnt pasta in the trash and dialing Pizza Boy, I continued. "Well, the beautiful, intelligent woman read the instructions on the back of the box:

Remove pie from carton and bake at 350 degrees. She took the pie out of the box—and out of the aluminum pie pan—and put it on the oven rack to bake.

"Then she went off to solve the nation's most pressing economic problems. Fifteen minutes later the kitchen filled up with smoke."

"You mean like the smoke you're trying to get rid of now?" asked Laura.

"No," I answered, "this smoke was thick. Black. Billowing."

"Like the forest fire on the news?"

"Yes, Laura, sort of like that. The pie had fallen apart, and peach filling oozed all over the electric heating element—and that started a fire. The husband had to buy a whole new oven and repaint the entire kitchen, which wasn't all that terrible since he had been promising to paint ever since they moved in.

"Now, the beautiful woman could've given up on her cooking aspirations, but besides being beautiful and multitalented, she also had perseverance."

At this point, Barry walked in and took over the story. "She also had a desire to show off for company. The long-suffering husband, after being hounded night and day to invite some friends over for dinner, did so to please his wife.

"And because he was a wise man, he gently encouraged his easily sidetracked wife (who often forgot about things she put in the oven) to serve takeout. Because she valued her pretty little neck, she bought a bucket of takeout chicken, put it on a fancy platter—even put little parsley doodads around it. Did the same for the mashed potatoes and coleslaw. But instead of getting a pie from the bakery like her wonderful husband suggested, the mule-headed woman tried once again to bake a pie.

"Much to the handsome husband's surprise, the pumpkin pie didn't look half bad. The woman had made it from scratch and everything, and she was very proud of that pie. I have to tell you, the handsome man (who at one time had to fight the girls off with a stick) was impressed too—at first. Remember, the man was not only handsome, he was also wise."

The girls leaned forward in their seats, spellbound. "The handsome man's wife served the pie on her elegant china dishes, all cut in perfect slices with dabs of whipped cream on each piece. All the dinner guests oohed and aahed—until they bit into it. Then, they all just sort of trembled. Bob started sweating, and his eyes bugged out. His wife, Anne, grabbed her glass of water and chug-a-lugged. Then she tried to grab Bob's water away from him! All their other guests were panting and fighting over each other's water too. It got ugly there for a minute."

"Did the woman put poison in the pie?" asked Laura.

"Not poison," I answered, "although her husband accused her of it. You see, the woman misread the directions and put in one cup of SALT instead of SUGAR."

Barry grabbed his throat and made gagging noises before continuing. "I'm happy to say that was the woman's last pie; unfortunately, it was not her last dessert. The woman once baked a huge chocolate cake for a church potluck dinner. She mixed up a bowlful of white peppermint icing and frosted it up all nice and fluffy. She did everything right, until she ran short of icing and discovered she didn't have enough powdered sugar to make more.

"So instead of bringing a half-frosted cake to the dinner or even buying a can of ready-made on the way there, the woman, who by then had lost her mind, mixed a tube of toothpaste in with the rest of the frosting."

At that, the girls began to howl at the thought of toothpaste icing, and I took up where Barry left off. "The beautiful, *resourceful* woman brought the cake to the potluck dinner, and everybody loved it. The only trouble was, afterward everyone had a sudden urge to rinse and spit. But that year her church had 80 percent fewer cavities than any other church in the area.

"The people were very happy and everyone loved the beautiful woman. But from then on, she was asked to bring napkins, not dessert, to potlucks.

That's when the beautiful woman decided that gourmet cooking was too much trouble, and she convinced her children that frozen french fries with grated cheese and canned chili over rice would make them grow strong and wise just like their dad and beautiful like their mom."

About that time the delivery man rang the doorbell, and a few minutes later we were all sitting at the table, fanning the last remaining puffs of smoke out of the kitchen and eating pizza.

"Good story, Mom," said Alison. "Good dinner, too. Best one this week."

"You outdid yourself, Nancy," said Barry.

"Yeah, Mom," Laura said through her bites of pepperoni. "I don't care what anyone says about you. Even though you're not like other moms, we still love you."

And the beautiful woman whispered, "Amen."

Not by French Fries Alone

One of the primary rules at my house is, "Don't tell anyone what I feed you." I particularly don't want other mothers to know, *especially* those who serve complete meals—daily.

I remember Laura coming home from eating at a friend's house one day, chattering about how they had meat *and* a salad *and* potatoes *and* vegetables *and* bread. "Why don't you do that, Mom?" she asked.

"I make all that," I told her. "Just not all at once."

Alison still recalls the time I served her and a friend canned pears, french fries with grated cheese, M&M's, and grape juice for dinner.

Sometimes I lie awake at night wondering what kind of domestic skills I'm passing on to them, and then I pray they'll find husbands who like to cook!

Cooking, however, is only one aspect of creating a home. As a mother, not only do I provide food for my family, but I also provide 24/7 training in what it means to make a home.

From me my children learn:

- table manners and how to make hospital corners on a bed
- love and commitment, honor, respect, and dignity…and where the salad forks go
- self-control and coping with disappointment
- traditions, charity, limits, and discipline

Home is the training ground where patience is tested, endurance is tried. It's where a child can make wrong choices, fall and fail, then get back up and find forgiveness. Home is where faith is practiced and godliness modeled. It's where a child can grow—body, soul, and spirit.

Training a child is a daunting task, an awesome responsibility. However, with power from the Spirit and wisdom from the Word of God, it's something I *can* do.

Maybe someday I'll even learn to cook—but it doesn't seem likely.

Digging Deeper

1. In *7 Habits of a Healthy Home,* Bill Carmichael says home needs to provide refuge, a place of formation, boundaries, a place of celebration, a place of connection, a legacy, and purpose. Think about each of these seven purposes as they pertain to your home. What have you done and what can you do to cultivate growth in each area? Ask the Lord to give you creative ideas to help you create a healthy home.

2. Read Psalm 127. How is it possible to labor in vain when it comes to building our homes? In my home, I have labored in vain whenever I've tried to do God's job: convicting of sin, changing hearts. I also labor in vain when I lie awake worrying about things I cannot control. What are ways *you* labor in vain? How does the Lord build a house?

3. In the midst of all the demands on our time with our children, it's easy to lose sight of our true goals. Yet daily struggles about

mundane things like chores and allowances can help serve our ultimate parenting goals. What are the most important skills you want your child to have before he or she leaves home? How can you work those into your daily routine?

4. Prayerfully choose a passage of Scripture as a life verse for yourself, your husband, and your children, and use it as a basis of prayer for them. For my family I use Isaiah 30:21, which says, "Whether you turn to the right or to the left, your ears will hear a voice behind you, saying, 'This is the way; walk in it.'"

"To some this world may seem like no place to bring up a child. And in some respects they are right: But we take that risk anyway with the comforting knowledge that it is not for this world that we prepare them."

—KAREN L. TORNBERG, quoted in *7 Habits of a Healthy Home*

Chapter 8

The Accidental Gardener

She considers a field and buys it;...
she plants a vineyard.

PROVERBS 31:16

The truth is, I've killed every plant I've ever touched. Any success at gardening is purely accidental. Like the time I spilled popcorn seeds and, on the way out to the trash, dropped some in the dirt on the side of the house. Without my even being aware of it, several popcorn plants grew to about five feet tall and produced two three-inch ears of popcorn. Unfortunately, the minute I touched them, they shriveled up and died between my anything-but-green thumbs.

My gardening dysfunction never bothered me until we moved to Florida a few years ago. Here, everything is green and lush, and gardening is a Way of Life—one that I've managed to ignore so far. That's not as simple as it may sound, what with the neighborhood garden patrol cruising by on their tractor lawn mowers to check for illicit cross-pollination and marauding cabbage worms. Not to mention the religious fervor over compost heaps and the raised eyebrows at the sight of a store-bought head of lettuce peeking out of anyone's grocery bag.

However, since digging into this whole Virtue adventure, I'd toyed with the idea of confronting my dysfunction and planting my own vineyard (or at least a vegetable garden). You could say the idea had been planted and was now germinating in my brain, ready to spring forth into new life.

Or you could say I felt left out in neighborhood gardening conversations. Whenever my neighbors get together, they start discussing soil chemistry and nematodes, and I end up feeling as welcome as root maggots in a radish patch. Besides, they possess something (or something possesses them) that makes their eyes light up and their hands smell like manure—and I wanted it.

Secretly at first, I began sneaking peeks at the gardening tracts they casually left in my mailbox. Then, more brazenly, I began asking questions. What does it mean to be nitrogen depleted? How deadly an enemy is the aphid? How can gardening change my life?

Just like remembering exactly where you were when you heard about President Kennedy's assassination, I remember the exact moment I was converted to gardening. I was at the market, picking over tomatoes at $1.79 a pound. Suddenly I realized if I were a Gardener, I could have my own tomatoes anytime I wanted—a whole salad for that matter—for the price I was about to pay for four Beefsteaks.

Well, tomatoes might have been the bait, but mulch was the line that reeled me in. Two women in the eggplant aisle were discussing mulch's benefits on strawberry plants. From the look of absolute rapture on their faces, I knew it was time for me to jump into the world of gardening with wholehearted abandon.

The next day I poured over Burpee seed catalogs and lusted after fifteen different varieties of zucchini. I studied how to maintain *esprit de corps* among the rows by companion planting. Having bought myself a spade, rake, hoe, and shovel, I set out to plow the back forty.

With my L. L. Bean straw gardening hat tied under my chin, I surveyed the situation in the side lot next to the house: eighteen live oak trees, seventy thousand waist-high shrubs, and weeds as far as the eye could see. After the first unyielding pull, I decided to leave the lot in all its untouched, natural grandeur and move my garden to a six-by-six plot at the side of the shed behind the house. It meant a few thousand less tomatoes, but at least the ground was already cleared. In fact, nothing had grown there in years.

According to my gardening handbook, the next step was to prepare the soil. The book said I needed a fragrant loam, loose and crumbly, easily cultivated and hospitable to roots. The soil needed to absorb water and drain quickly, with lots of air space to circulate vital oxygen and soil bacteria. I got down on my knees and plunged my hands into the dirt.

Truthfully, I don't know packed silt from acidic peat (dirt is just dirt in my opinion), but since I was embarking on a horticultural spiritual journey, I decided to consult the neighborhood G.E.s (Gardening Experts). They descended on my plot and offered their sage advice.

"Mix the dirt with grass clippings, cedar chips, and finely chopped leaves," suggested one expert.

"Never till organic material directly into soil in its uncomposted state," warned another.

Another sung the praises of red worms, while two others argued the pros and cons of peat moss.

The only thing everyone agreed on was manure.

Ah, manure. At the mention of that semimiraculous substance, the Experts threw back their heads in rapture. At their unanimous suggestion, I chose a light yet haughty vintage pig dung and mixed it into my soil. While their eyes practically rolled back in their heads, frankly, it did nothing for me.

Maybe I missed something. I mean, despite its reputation for nutritional excellence, it still smelled like…well, like pig dung. Still, I'd committed myself for the long haul, and if that meant pig dung up to my elbows, so be it.

Next came seed planting time. That was easy: Open the seed packages and let them fly. (I went for the tossed garden salad effect rather than the usual silver bells and cockle shells and pretty maids all in a row.) Then throw on some mulch, sprinkle a little fertilizer, spritz a little water. I still didn't see what the big deal was all about.

And then I composted.

Replenishing, renourishing compost. A pile of coffee grounds and carrot peelings, fruit rinds and eggshells, pet hair and barnyard manure. I kept it moist; I turned it often. It was the lifeline to my garden—and my garden, the lifeline back to me. Morning, noon, and night I added to my pile, at times swiping the food off my family's plates.

"We'll get it back a thousandfold," I'd say, taking a half-eaten corncob out of my daughter's hand.

For days and weeks on end, I composted and mulched with all my heart. Once tiny green sproutlets pushed through the soil, I added weeding and fertilizing to my list of daily duties. And then when my plants started bearing fruit, well, let me just say, any doubts I may have had about the gardening Way of Life were dispelled.

"Ah, yes," I said to the (albeit still green) fruit of my labor, "I can already taste the sweetness of Virtue. This will push me up and over the top—why, this gardening stuff may even cancel out all my previous Virtue deficiencies!"

Self-satisfied and dirty-fingernailed, I forsook everyone and everything else and devoted my whole existence to nurturing my teeny green tomatoes, miniature zucchinis, and wee little eggplants.

Then disaster struck.

One morning I found the telltale signs of midnight marauders (raccoons): a dozen ears of corn and several heads of lettuce, brutally plucked, their remains scattered across the yard. Every morning after that I'd find similar evidence: footprints, discarded corn silk, an occasional thank-you note.

Harvesttime came none too soon. The honeymoon glow of my first days as a Gardener had long since worn off. The deep sense of purpose and commitment hadn't left, but the everyday walk had taken its toll on me, not to mention my family. They were tired of my talk of "pH balance" and "nutrient density." Tired too of fragrant, loamy footprints on the carpet and the smell of peat moss in my hair.

When Harvest Day finally did arrive, it found me standing ready with baskets and barrels and forty dozen quart canning jars waiting in anticipation for the fruit—make that vegetables—of my labor. All the summer sweat mingling with the dirt, all the days of swatting mosquitoes and standing watch against crows and slugs were about to pay off.

Eagerly, proudly, I harvested all afternoon, discerningly discarding the imperfect and inedible. The raccoons had eaten all the corn; worms had destroyed all the tomatoes. The radishes and radicchio tried some illicit cross-pollinating and came up barren. The cantaloupes tried but couldn't.

Still, I managed to fill every room in the house with bounty from my garden: 183 eggplants.

The Gardeners had been right. The satisfaction of reaping a bountiful harvest was like nothing else on earth. I could compare it only to the joy of learning that something I'd said or written had impacted another person's walk with God. It was like catching a surprising glimpse of Laura in her room studying her Sunday school lesson or overhearing Alison telling a friend how faith in Christ makes a difference in her life. These are the real fruits of my planting.

As I cradled an eggplant in my arms and thought back on all my months of toil, I knew it had been worth it. It reminded me that even though we may sow some seeds in tears, we will reap a harvest of joy (Psalm 126:5).

And maybe even eggplants, I thought as I walked from room to room, admiring the product of my own two hands (not to mention $859 in equipment, seeds, etc.). Unfortunately, there was one minor glitch: No one in my family likes eggplant, and the likelihood of getting anyone (myself included) to eat it was akin to seeing a donkey fly.

Still, it wasn't a total loss. Luckily for me, eggplant makes *great* compost.

Secrets of the Soil

Recently I polled some gardening friends about the most important elements in a healthy garden. At the top of the list were good soil, sufficient water, and sunshine. Take any of these away and your plants will die. But the process starts with good soil. Good soil mix determines the richness or weakness of the plant growth—just as the condition of your heart will determine the quality of your faith.

If the soil consists of only one element or if the same crop has been planted year after year, the soil needs enrichment.

> Make every effort to add to your faith goodness; and to
> goodness, knowledge; and to knowledge, self-control;
> and to self-control, perseverance; and to perseverance,
> godliness; and to godliness, brotherly kindness; and to
> brotherly kindness, love. (2 Peter 1:5-7)

If the soil is rocky or if it has fungus or cinch bugs, the plants will die. Steps must be taken to eradicate these hazards from your soil.

> But now you must rid yourselves of all such things as
> these: anger, rage, malice, slander, and filthy language
> from your lips. Do not lie to each other, since you
> have taken off your old self with its practices. (Colos-
> sians 3:8-9)

If the soil is hard-packed and hasn't been tilled in a while, the roots can't grow. The soil needs to be broken up so the roots can take in nutrients.

> This is what the LORD says…: "Break up your
> unplowed ground and do not sow among thorns."
> (Jeremiah 4:3)

Once the soil is healthy, seed can be sown, and with proper watering, careful cultivation, and diligent weed control, plus plenty of sunshine, a gardener can expect a bumper crop at harvesttime. Then, as the prophet Isaiah writes, "[We] will be called oaks of righteousness, a planting of the LORD for the display of his splendor" (Isaiah 61:3). Healthy…fruitful… with roots grown deep.

Digging Deeper

1. Think about your favorite fruit. How do you like to eat it—raw, cooked, in a pie or salad? What do you know about how it grows and how it's harvested? Now think about the term "a fruitful life." What does that typically mean?

2. In *Stepping Out on Faith*, Jerry Falwell lists the characteristics of spiritual fruit: (1) It's given to all believers. (2) It produces spiritual character. (3) It is "fruit"—singular—meaning you can't have one characteristic without the others. (4) It is permanent. (5) It grows internally. Galatians 5:22-23 describes the fruit of God's Spirit in a believer. List each "piece of fruit" and, using a dictionary or a thesaurus, write out their definitions. Now, using a concordance, research what the Bible says about each of these fruitful qualities.

3. What does the Bible say about how fruit is produced in a Christian? Read the following passages and record what you learn:

John 15:5; 1 Corinthians 3:6-9; Philippians 1:9-11; Colossians 1:10. How have you seen the evidence of spiritual fruit in your own life? What are you doing within your family to help prepare for a spiritual harvest?

4. Although it seems contrary to logic, the way to increase a plant's productivity is to cut off its branches. Likewise, God often trims our lives in order to produce more and better quality fruit. Read these passages to learn how he does it: Deuteronomy 8:1-9; Romans 8:28; Hebrews 12:1-13; James 1:1-4. How have you been "pruned" by God? What fruit have you produced because of those pruning experiences? (If you're going through a painful time of pruning right now, remember that God isn't angry with you but is doing it out of love. Also, he promises sufficient grace to endure every trial.)

~

"My azalea bush was struggling. Colorless leaves hung on limp branches with sparse flowers. I tenderly cut back every branch, assuring myself how lopping off lifeless branches would pave the way for new flowers next spring. Suddenly, I realized how lovingly and gingerly God removes old branches from my life so I can sprout new growth. I wasn't punishing the azalea because it hadn't yielded enough flowers; I was doing everything I could to help it grow because I'm fond of the little bush and want it to do well."

—SUSAN M. SMITH, "How Does Your Garden Grow?" *Today's Christian Woman*

Chapter 9

For Your Thighs Only

Her arms are strong for her tasks.
PROVERBS 31:17

I'm outnumbered in our family when it comes to horseplay. When every-one starts playing punch-for-punch or living room tackle, I wimp out—just fall on the floor and cover myself or fake an appendicitis attack so I won't get clobbered.

When we have "show me your muscle" contests, I always lose. No matter how hard I tense, my triceps still jiggle, and everyone laughs. As Laura says, "Mom, you're just not macho."

With her words echoing in my ears, I opened my Bible and groaned. "Oh no. Her arms are strong for her tasks!" Not exactly what I wanted to read right then. Some people have bad hair days; I was having a bad body day.

Physically drained from...I don't know what, since I hadn't done any-thing, I sighed, dragged myself over to the couch, and flipped through my medical reference guide, hoping to find a name for the way I was feeling. I found it. I'd contracted the dreaded "I Can't See My Toes, Let Alone Touch Them" Syndrome.

I had all the symptoms. Lethargy, apathy, a stomach that hung down to my knees. Arm flab that flapped in the wind. I got winded running up my credit card. Had to take a nap before bedtime.

My zip was zapped; my pep had pooped.

I should have suspected something was wrong that morning when I stepped out of the shower only to have Barry survey my naked body and shake his head saying, "You poor thing."

Hmmm, Mr. Proverbs probably never said that to his wife, I thought as I put the reference book back on the shelf. *It's time to get into shape.* It's not that I wasn't in shape. It's just that the shape I was in was round...and soft...and squishy.

I began my new Get in Shape program the way I begin any major lifestyle change, by reading up on the subject and putting together all necessary supplies and equipment. Some people call it stalling; I call it "research."

After I'd gathered all the fitness books and magazines I could get my wimpy arms around, I read about isokinetic resistance and isolating muscle groups. I studied plié squats and leg curls. Then I bought a Thigh Master, a Belly Buster, and a Rump Rectifier, watched the television exercise shows daily, and bought my own exercise videos. At $19.95 each I now own *Buns of Steel, Abs of Granite,* and *Pecs of Concrete.* I already had Saddlebags of Jell-O.

The only problem was, in order to get the maximum benefit—or even the minimum benefit—out of any of these products, you have to actually use them. Oh yeah.

So I moaned and I groaned. I sweated and I panted. Then, once I got the boxes open, I took a much-needed M&M's and Diet Pepsi break.

After three days of strenuous box opening and arduous candy eating, I still didn't see any results. (A clear violation of truth in advertising.) Not one to give up easily, I moved on to Phase Two of my new exercise regimen: The Outfit.

I'd seen The Outfit in all the magazines. First you put on girdlelike, sucks-in-your-gut tights, preferably skin-colored (that is, if your skin is the color of my father-in-law's Cadillac).

Next comes the sports bra that slips over your head and twists around your neck, cutting off your air supply as you try to find the armholes. (I'm told that's good for your cardiovascular breathing.)

After that, bike shorts and then the leotard. I have to warn you to watch out for the ones that are missing parts of the back. Avoid these. The only cheeks we want exposed are the ones on our faces.

Over all that you throw on a huge tank top that covers up all the lumps, rolls, and sags. And then the *pièce de résistance:* the matching socks and the sneakers that cost roughly the same as a mortgage payment.

Once I had The Outfit, I needed a place to wear it.

I went to The Gym.

I'd heard about these places before, but I'd never actually been inside one. As I walked inside, I was greeted by a six-foot-three blonde with biceps the likes of which I'd never seen on any man.

The blonde introduced herself as "Debi-with an-i."

After the preliminaries of taking my name and all the money in my bank account, Debi-with-an-i showed me around the gym. And then the part I'd been dreading: She whipped out her tape measure (gulp!), TOOK MY MEASUREMENTS, then called out the numbers into a loudspeaker. For the hearing impaired, she also simultaneously flashed the numbers on a screen in blinking lights.

Not yet finished humiliating me, she led me to a room lined with (magnifying) mirrors; low, plastic, benchlike steps; and about two dozen tight-stomached, lean-legged nymphets wearing those leotards I warned you about.

"Just watch what I do and follow along," said Debi-with-an-i as she put a step bench in front of me and turned on the music. At that point, all the nymphets jumped up and whooped and hopped and bounced in place, clapping their hands.

"I can do this," I said and bounced around a bit myself. Then everyone started stepping up on their benches and then down. And then up and back down. And then sideways and then backward. And then they moved their arms, up and down, back and forth—never missing a beat, never ceasing to whoop.

"Pump it, ladies," shouted Debi-with-an-i. "Now double-time!"

By the time the first song ended, I was exhausted—and all I'd done was tie my shoes and watch. For the next song, however, I got up on my step. At the next, I got down. During the next song, I managed to get up twice and down three times (I slipped) and even to move my arms a few times. By the fifth song, I'd had enough and went home to nurse my aching calf muscles and soothe my tired arms.

Just as I was about to step into the bathtub, the phone rang. It was Kathy.

"Sweetie, I've been sooo worried about you," she oozed. (Really.) "It's been simply months and months since we talked. You've given up on your silly Virtuous Woman thing, haven't you?"

I rubbed my sore arm. "Of course not! Why would you think that?"

"Come on, tell me the truth. Don't you think you've bitten off way more than you can chew?"

I rubbed my other arm. "No, I don't think so. Do you?" I rubbed my left calf and for a brief moment considered returning to life in its unvirtuous, natural state. At least then I wouldn't have to continue exercising my arms.

I heard a *psshhh* on the other end of the line, then a moment of silence. Finally Kathy spoke. "No, but…well, you know, I'm only trying to help. So tell me, what verse are you working on now? Maybe I can give you some advice."

I winced as I tried making a muscle. "Her arms are strong for her tasks."

The phone went silent again.

"Kathy? Are you still there?"

"Sweetie," she said (only it sounded more like "Sa-weeeeet-tee"), "now what I'm about to say is strictly out of love: You'll never make this one. I've seen your arms. *I've seen your thighs.* Why don't you just stop all this non-sense and do something worthwhile? Like crossword puzzles."

This time my end of the phone went silent. Maybe this Drive to Be Virtuous really was nonsense. Maybe I was never meant to be a modern-day VW. Would my family be better off if I stopped my Pursuit? Would God be mad if I did? Was there no hope for my flabby arms? And what about my thighs?

"Kathy," I said, "even if I wanted to, I can't give up. If not for myself, then I have to continue for my family's sake. The girls need a Virtuous Mom. Barry needs a Virtuous Wife. I need strong arms." I hit my fist on the kitchen counter. "Besides, if Gideon could do it, then so can I."

"Sweetie, you're babbling. What does Gideon have to do with your puny arm muscles?"

"Don't you remember in the book of Judges where it talks about Gideon and how he led the Israelites against Midian? Well, when God called him, he was hiding out in a wine press, trying to thresh wheat. The angel of the Lord hailed him as a mighty warrior and told him, 'Go in the strength you have.'"

"Sweetie, I still don't get it. Where do your flabby arms fit in?"

"God chose Gideon in spite of his lack of physical strength or power. Or more correctly, because of it. That way, God could be strong through Gideon's weakness. If he could do it for Gideon, surely he could do it for me. Maybe he can even build up these saggy arms."

"Well, sweetie, I suppose you're right. And if you feel you must con-tinue, then you must." Then, with her customary "ta ta," she hung up, and I went back to my (now cold) bath.

The next day, armed with fresh resolve (and smelling of Bengay), I struggled back into The Outfit and returned to The Gym for another shot at strengthening my arms (and legs) for my tasks. This time Debi-with-an-i put me on a computerized stationary bike. After placing my feet in the stirrups, she hooked me up to a monitor that allowed me to watch a panel of little lights in front of me.

"The higher the line of lights," explained Miss I, "the harder you're working." As she set the timer for thirty minutes and bounced away, I started pedaling, all the while picturing Gideon blowing his trumpet in battle and the VW lifting buckets of water and pedaling on her exercise bike.

I pedaled with all my Gideonlike strength (not much) until I was exhausted—all of two minutes—never once seeing a single light go higher than "wimp speed." After that I coasted the rest of the twenty-eight minutes. The spirit was willing, but the muscles were oh-so-weak.

The next day Debi-with-an-i had me work with free weights. They may have been free, but they were still heavy. Luckily, I dropped one on my toe and went home early. Unfortunately, I was fine the next day and felt compelled to go back. This time Debi-with-an-i handed me a chart and told me we were going to use the machines.

Now, I'd seen the people on the machines, and to me it looked like the machines weren't doing any of the work. What kind of machine is that? I ask you.

She strapped me into a chairlike device with a padded arm that crushed my chest, then told me to bend forward. "This will tighten up those loose abs," she said, eyeing my middle.

Now, correct me if I'm wrong, but I don't remember reading anything about the Virtuous Woman having tight abs. Still, I'd paid my membership fee. What could it hurt to try?

It hurt my abs.

"Uuuunnnn, uuuunnn, uuunnn," I moaned. After three or four minutes of moaning, I'd managed to bend once all the way down and once back up. That's when I decided my abs could stay loose, called it a day, and went home.

On Friday, the last day of my week-long exercise regimen, I graduated to the treadmill. Now *that* I liked. An automatic moving sidewalk is my kind of machine. Debi showed me how to turn it on and gave me a pair of hand weights to help build up my arms. I walked, I pumped my arms, I sweat like I'd never sweat before. Oddly enough, it felt good.

Look at me, Mrs. P! My arms may be weak and my legs sore, but I can do this! I can do all things through Christ who gives me the strength—just like you.

By the time my thirty minutes were up, I felt ready once again to conquer the world (in spirit only—my legs felt like boiled linguine, and I couldn't wait to get home to a hot bath and my tube of Bengay). Even so, after only a week of exercise, I did notice some improvement, especially in my arms. When I stopped off at the minimart on my way home for a celebratory Diet Pepsi and bag of M&M's, I could open them both with only one hand.

The Strength of a Wimp

One of my favorite Bible characters is Gideon, son of Joash the Abiezrite. Gideon was a big coward. His story opens in Judges 6, where we find him threshing wheat in a wine press while hiding from the Midianites.

The angel of the Lord appeared to him and said, "The LORD is with you, mighty warrior." Then the Lord told him, "Go in the strength you have and save Israel out of Midian's hand."

Gideon basically replied, "Say what? You've got the wrong guy. I'm trying to *hide* from the Midianites! How do you expect me to save Israel from them?"

The Lord answered, "I will be with you."

Duh.

That's always the "how" part of anything the Lord asks us to do, no matter how seemingly impossible it sounds.

How can I handle this wayward child, Lord?

I will be with you.

How can I love this husband I'm not sure I even like anymore?

I will be with you.

I have cancer, Lord.

I will be with you.

My child's in jail, Lord—I don't think I can handle much more.

I will be with you.

Judges 7 says Gideon defeated the Midianites, but actually, God did. All Gideon did was hold a torch and blow a trumpet, and God caused Gideon's enemies to kill each other.

How could a wimp become a warrior? The Lord was with him; the Lord was his strength.

Duh.

Digging Deeper

1. What is society's definition of strength? What is considered weakness? Who is the strongest woman you know? Why would you describe her that way?

2. God seems to delight in paradoxes: The first are last, the weak are strong. In the following Scripture passages, identify the person's weakness: Genesis 17:15-27; 18:10-14; 21:1-7; Genesis 29:15–30:24; Exodus 3:10–4:17; Ruth 1:1-22; 4:13-17; 2 Kings 4:1-7; Jeremiah 1:5-12; Matthew 1:18-25; Luke 1:26-38; Philippians 1:12-19. How did God turn each person's weakness into strength?

3. What are some of your weaknesses? How has God shown his strength through your weaknesses? Take a moment to think about a current weakness, then ask God to change it to a strength for his glory. (See 2 Corinthians 12:1-10.)

4. Consider the following quote:

> A person who calls himself frank and candid can very easily find himself becoming tactless and cruel.
>
> A person who prides himself on being tactful can find eventually that he has become evasive and deceitful.
>
> A person with firm convictions can become pigheaded.
>
> A person who is inclined to be temperate and judicious can sometimes turn into someone with weak convictions and banked fires of resolution....
>
> Loyalty can lead to fanaticism. Caution can become timidity. Freedom can become license. Confidence can become arrogance. Humility can become servility.
>
> All these are ways in which strength can become weakness.

—DORE SCHARY, "Bits and Pieces"

Can you think of other "strengths" that can become weaknesses?

"There is sublime joy in holy boasting of the power of God in a life that is totally dependent on him. There is sublime peace in accepting the sufficiency of God's grace by allowing him to be strong in us where we are weak."

—MARIE CHAPIAN, *Women's Devotional Bible*

Chapter 10

The Back-Door Gift

She sees that her trading is profitable.

PROVERBS 31:18

My philosophy concerning money is simple: Give me some, and I'll spend it, then hold my hand out for more. It's worked well so far, first with my mom and dad, then with my husband. So you can understand my surprise—my utter mouth-hanging-open disbelief—the day I showed Barry my verse du jour and asked him for money so I could go out and trade profitably at the mall *and he said no.*

Just like that. No. NO! Not only that, he added some lame excuse like it was for my own good. Well, you'll be happy to know, because I've reached a certain degree of maturity, I let it pass. (Besides, my birthday was a few days away, and I didn't want to hurt my chances at getting a really great present from Barry.)

During the days leading up to my birthday, Barry (as always) kept dropping hints about his gift to me—only these hints were different from his usual "They're round and silver and you wear them in your ears" type hints.

"It's something you've wanted for a long time," he said one day as I stood in the bathroom doorway watching him shave.

"A dozen red roses? Liposuction? My gums to stop receding?"

"Not even close," he said and hopped in the shower. Over the glass door he shouted, "Here's another clue: You're going to love it because it'll help you in this Virtue thing you're working on. BUT you're also going to hate it."

Normally I can guess his gifts days before I get them, but this one stumped me. While he showered, I searched all his not-so-secret hiding places throughout the house for a package, a receipt—anything for a clue—but came up empty handed.

"I know what you're doing out there!" he called. "And you're not going to find it."

This went on every day until my birthday. That evening after work he walked through the back door (something he doesn't usually do) and into the kitchen, grinning. "Are you ready for your present now?" he asked.

I closed my eyes and held out my hands. And held them and held them and held them.

"Surprise!" he yelled.

Yeah, I was surprised. He'd given me nothing. Well, sort of.

"I thought long and hard about what you really want," he said, then took a deep breath, "and I've decided to give you as your birthday present…responsibility, independence, and freedom."

My turn to grin. "No, really. What did you get me?"

"I told you: responsibility, independence, and freedom."

I mulled it over for a while but still didn't get it. Finally I took a guess. "Concert tickets? I've heard of R.E.M. and INXS, but not RIF."

While I searched the house for a gift box or shopping bag, Barry followed me around, still grinning.

"No pink terry-cloth bathrobe from Victoria's Secret?" I called from inside the hall closet.

"Nope."

"No jewelry?" I asked from under the kitchen sink.

He just stood there, shaking his head. When I'd looked everywhere twice, he said, "Hold your hands back out."

I did.

"What usually happens when you do that?"

"Somebody puts money in them, and I spend it."

"Now what have you been wanting for the last few years?"

I skimmed my mental wish list: clothes, trinkets, baubles, real estate. Neither R nor I nor F was on it. Except…

Over the past few years I'd been thinking a lot about how Barry took care of everything for me and how I lived somewhere off in La-La Land, oblivious to the real cost of living. But as for RIF? I'd never mentioned them, except maybe a fleeting comment about never having lived on my own and how if I were ever left alone I'd probably end up eating birdseed and living under the freeway somewhere.

"So, how do I get this responsibility, independence, and freedom? Hmmm?" I asked him.

He spelled it out for me: a budget of my very own. From that day forward, no more holding out my little hands for money, just a set amount every payday for food, gas and maintenance for my car, and extras. Sounded okay to me—until he went further.

"Also, if you want to go to the gym, get a haircut, or have lunch with your friends, you need to budget for it. AND if you use money out of savings, you have to replace it. AND with money you earn from your writing, you have to set aside enough to pay your own taxes." He paused, then said with a stupid Cheshire cat grin, "Happy Birthday!"

"Happy Birthday? So when do I get to the 'I'm going to love it' part?"

"You'll know," he said.

I knew for sure I'd already reached the "you'll hate it" part. I mean, why couldn't he just buy me a CD player or some new underwear? I'd settle for a bottle of cheap perfume and a bouquet of day-old carnations.

Maybe this venture into RIFdom won't be too bad, I thought. I still had a trick or two left.

"Oh, by the way," Barry interrupted my plotting, "no more raiding my wallet."

Rats! Wallet raiding had been my number-one trick. That left only pleading, wheedling, and cajoling, but noting the look of delight and determination on Barry's face, I kissed those babies good-bye.

I may have started out with a whimper, but that changed to a full-fledged whine when payday rolled around and I got a look at what I had to work with. "How do you expect me to maintain my standard of living?" I whined as Barry handed me a check.

"You're creative," he answered.

"I don't want to be creative. I want money to grow on trees." But creative I am, and like it or not, creative I would be. Mainly because he'd left me no choice.

The third thing I did (first I set aside my tithe, then I cried) was open my Bible to see if the VW ever had this problem.

"Of course not," I said, skimming the text. "She was probably her neighborhood Coupon-Clipping Queen. She probably bought generic corn chips and bargain-brand salsa. She probably made her own dishwasher soap."

So I determined to step up to the challenge. I would become the frugalest and the tightwaddiest. A budgeteer extraordinaire.

I started by clipping coupons. I'd heard about people who get a year's worth of groceries for only eighty-seven cents by using coupons. I'd seen women carrying around huge file folders and calculators in the market. I can do that too, I decided.

And I did.

Over the next couple of weeks, I saved nearly twenty-two dollars on stuff we never, ever buy and hardly even like and seventy-five cents on something I'd never even heard of. I carried my file folders around and held up long lines at the checkout counters while I leafed through my coupons, all in pursuit of saving thirty cents on cat food and fifty cents on air freshener.

I also discovered that if you buy food nobody likes, it lasts longer. No one's in a hurry to gobble up Raspberry Choco Krisps or canned okra.

Next I tried buying generically. Yellow-labeled canned green beans, yellow-labeled cream corn. Toasted oat cereal in yellow bags and a processed imitation cheese-flavored product in yellow boxes.

I went one step further and shopped the dented can/smashed box warehouses, buying things called Tastee Yummy and Maxi Fine. I split rolls of two-ply toilet paper into two rolls and gave everyone in the family their own weekly portion. I cut fabric softener sheets in half. Then in thirds. Then down to postage stamp size. Finally I decided rough clothes build character and stopped buying dryer sheets altogether.

One of my favorite tricks (which you can't reveal to my kids, or they'll have gross-out attacks): When everyone leaves the house in the mornings, I mix up a batch of powdered milk and add it to the jugs of "real" milk.

I embraced my austerity with wholehearted abandon, gathering bits of soap from the sink counters and shower floors and mushing them into odd-shaped globs to reuse. I dug through sofa cushions and checked under car mats for stray coins. I chased pennies through parking lots when they rolled out of my purse. I rationed grapes and declared water to be our family's new beverage of choice. I even started making Clean Out the Refrigerator Soup.

I made do. I did without. Most novel of all, I trusted God to meet my needs. And I never once raided my husband's wallet or held out my little hand to him (unless it was for holding), even during weeks when my checkbook and gas tank both registered empty three days before payday. Those I called my "Adventures in Faith" days, although my daughters referred to them as, "Oh no, looks like we can't go to the movies" days or "Mom's in the Poorhouse" days. Barry called them "Uh-oh. Beans and Rice Again" days.

We survived them. We're still surviving them. Besides, to my knowledge, nobody has ever died from lack of movies or an overdose of pinto beans.

All in all, Barry was right about his odd choice of a birthday gift. And except for a few bad haircuts I inflicted on myself and a crying jag or two over missed clearance sales at the mall, I did okay. Let me change that to present tense—I'm doing okay. Seems this wasn't just a one-shot deal but a lifetime change.

And you know what? There's always just enough for our needs and occasionally a little more. How about that?

Hey, Mrs. P., my trading is profitable too!

As I write this, I'm thinking about my next birthday. Since I already have responsibility, independence, and freedom, what more can I ask for? How about patience?

One can never have enough of that, you know.

What Do I Really Need?

I own a pair of three-dollar pants. I couldn't *not* buy them—they were marked down from forty-five dollars. Even the Proverbs Thirty-One Woman wouldn't have passed them up. However, I didn't have anything to wear with them, so *of course* I needed to buy a black, collarless jacket *and* a white camisole with Battenburg lace *and* a pair of black pumps *and* a pair of gold hoop earrings, all to go with my three-dollar pants.

By the time I was finished shopping, my three-dollar pants outfit ended up costing close to one hundred fifty dollars. The irony is, it's so warm where I live in Florida that I rarely get the opportunity to wear it. My bargain three-dollar pants weren't a bargain after all.

In *Lost in the Money Maze,* author Patricia Rushford writes about the "malling of America." She says we shop as recreation, buying things we don't need. She advises developing a godly viewpoint by asking, "What do I really need?" and "Am I managing God's resources his way?"

The woman of Proverbs 31 saw that her trading was profitable. She was prudent, resourceful. As with the rest of her household duties, she managed the assets with which God had entrusted her in a way that honored him. In modern terms, she didn't blow her money at the mall, using shopping as recreation, and she didn't stuff her closets with stuff she didn't need. I suspect she used her money and possessions as tools for ministry and not as ends unto themselves.

Do you want to be wealthy? Then delight yourself in the Lord, for true riches are never found in the abundance of things, which only rust and fade and shrink in the dryer. Instead, true riches are found in the abundance of God's grace.

That beats a pair of three-dollar pants any day.

Digging Deeper

1. How much time do you spend shopping in an average week? How much of that is out of necessity? How much is recreational? Do your shopping habits create friction between you and your spouse?

2. Read the following scriptures: Proverbs 30:8-9; Matthew 6:19-21; Luke 12:15-21; 1 Timothy 6:6-10; Hebrews 13:5. What do they say about our attitudes toward money and treasures?

3. The Bible cautions believers against unbalanced lifestyles and thinking. The Lord promises to supply all our needs (Philippians 4:19), not necessarily all our wants. Read Matthew 25:14-30. What does this parable teach about how to manage the money and resources that God gives us? How can you apply this to your financial situation?

4. How many times have you walked around the mall with discontent, wanting more, more, more? One of the best cures for discontent is thanksgiving. Using Acts 14:17 as a model, write a prayer giving thanks to God for all that he has provided for you. A sample prayer might be: *Lord, you have shown your kindness for me in every season, whether I've had plenty or what I thought was not enough. But even in the leanest times I have always had enough,*

always more than enough. More than filling my life with things, you have filled my heart with joy, and I am satisfied. Help me to remember that! (I forget so easily.) I know I can trust you to always provide, because you are my Father, the Great Shepherd, and my Gracious King. Amen.

"I'm convinced that giving away and saving money are the antidotes for overspending. They produce a lasting feeling of well-being and satisfaction that spending money can never satisfy long-term."

—MARY HUNT, *The Bible for Today's Christian Woman*

Chapter 11

Fingers Flexed and
Itching to Serve

She opens her arms to the poor and
extends her hands to the needy.

PROVERBS 31:20

L ike you, I want my life to count. I want to make a difference. That's
exactly what I told my pastor the day I went to see him at his office.

"Look at these," I said, rolling up my sleeves to show him my biceps.
"And these." I flexed my fingers and wiggled them in front of his face.

"Very impressive," he said. "But can you rub your stomach and pat your
head at the same time?"

"Pastor, you don't get it." I opened my Bible and showed him Proverbs
31. "See here? It says in verse 20 that the VW opens her arms to the poor
and extends her hands to the needy. That's what I want to do. I've been
doing arm and finger exercises for weeks now, and it's time for me to put
them to work. I just don't know what I can do."

"Hmmm, what are your gifts, your talents?" he asked.

I was afraid he'd ask me that. While the *Jeopardy* theme song played in
the background, I knit my brows together and thought. I struck the same
pose as Rodin's *The Thinker* and thought some more. I twiddled my thumbs,
then rubbed my stomach and patted my head while I thought even more.

Finally I snapped my fingers. "I'm good at Trivial Pursuit. I can balance seven empty soda cans on the way out to the recycling bin. I can recite all the words to the 'Fly Away, Little Birdie' song that I learned in kindergarten. I can—"

Just as I was about to say, "I can spit a cherry pit into the sink from across the kitchen," the pastor interrupted.

"I may be wrong, but I don't think there's a big demand for any of those gifts." He tapped his finger on his chin for a minute. "I know! How about cleaning the carpet in the sanctuary? We're having a church workday this Saturday, and we need someone to run the carpet cleaner."

"I can do that." Actually, I wasn't sure whether I could or not, but I'd seen it done. Besides, how difficult could it be?

On Saturday I found out. And truly, running the carpet cleaner was easy. Chasing it down the center aisle, watching it nick the pews, and having the cord pull out of the wall socket and whip around the sanctuary until it hit and dented the narthex door—*that* was hard.

Thankfully, my pastor is a gracious man who cared more about my feelings than about anything I may have damaged. When he heard the commotion and saw the scratched wood all over the church, he suggested I go right home and take things easy.

"But I want to help," I protested.

"You've helped enough," he said as he escorted me to my car.

"I only wanted to help," I muttered as I drove out the church driveway. I muttered all the way down the street and continued to mutter as I pulled into the grocery store parking lot and marched into the market.

"How can I achieve Virtue unless I open my arms to the needy?" I murmured as I pulled two shopping carts apart for an elderly woman behind me. Up and down the aisles I traveled, hoping for inspiration but coming out of the store with only a gallon of milk, three cans of tomato soup, and a bag of cat litter.

I must help the needy, I thought the next day and sat down to make a list of potential recipients of my charity: Judy, a woman with a new baby; the community soup kitchen at a local church; and Joe, a man whose house had been damaged by a recent flood. Then, with open arms and extended hands, I set out to help.

Unfortunately, every place I went that day I arrived too late. Someone had already arranged to deliver meals to Judy; someone else had cleaned her house. Not only that, when I knocked on her door, she was on her way to take a shower and the baby was asleep. "You can come in and listen for the baby while I'm in the shower," she said.

So I did. I sat for about fifteen minutes, then when Judy got out of the shower, the baby cried, and she went over to pick him up. That was that, and I left.

Disappointed, I moved on to the next item on my list: the soup kitchen. Again, somebody had beaten me to it. All the fun jobs were taken, and one too many cooks (me) would only spoil the broth. Besides, they had already started serving. The only thing left for me to do was grab a plate of food and sit down to eat.

I found a spot next to a lady with two squirmy little boys whose busy hands were preventing their mom from enjoying her meal. When I sat down, she offered a half smile as her boys' attention turned to me and the pads of paper and two pens I took out of my purse.

The three of us drew pictures of Mickey Mouse and took turns playing tick-tack-toe while the woman finished eating. Then she put her head down on the table and fell asleep! I didn't know what else to do, so I took the boys out to the church's playground and pushed them on the swings—all the while churning inside because I'd missed my chance to help serve in the kitchen.

After I handed the boys back to their mother, refreshed from her nap, I went over to help Joe with his flood damage repairs—and met with disappointment again. All the heavy work had been done earlier while I was playing with those boys. I ended up standing at Joe's desk, of all things, peeling apart sheets of postage stamps that had gotten wet, while Joe sat and talked to me about all that had happened during the storm.

This is so trivial. I came here to help, and all I'm doing is setting out stamps to dry.

Thoroughly frustrated at my failure to find a way to open my arms and extend my hands, I peeled the last sheet apart, hugged my friend Joe, then went home.

When I walked in the door, I immediately noticed the green light flashing on my answering machine. My pastor had called to say a van was leaving from the church parking lot the following morning for a one-day mission trip. If I wanted to help distribute blankets and sandwiches to the street people of a nearby city, I should meet the mission team at 9 A.M.

At last! My itchy fingers will finally have a place to extend! I wiggled my fingers the rest of the evening, set my alarm, and went to bed.

Although I awoke the next morning in plenty of time, I still ran late, what with getting everyone off to school and work on time. Not only that, but my car was low on fuel, and I had to stop at the gas station. As I pumped, a woman approached me. *Oh, no, what does she want?* From the looks of her Anne Klein suit, I assumed she wanted to sell me a house or manage my nonexistent investment portfolio.

"Excuse me," she said. "I hate to bother you—I never do this—but can I trouble you for a ride? This is so embarrassing, but I just had a fight with my husband. He left me here and just took off. He's got my purse—I don't even have money for a phone call."

I looked at my watch. I was running late and didn't have any time to spare. "I'm sorry," I told her. "I really can't. But here's fifty cents for the phone."

She thanked me; I paid for my gas, then sped away, knowing I'd have to roll through every stop sign and exceed every speed limit in order to make up for the time I'd just wasted. Yet, even though I violated as many traffic regulations as I could, I arrived too late.

"Lord, what is the problem here?" I cried out. Defeated and frustrated once again, I turned around to go home. As I passed the gas station, I noticed the same woman I'd met earlier.

Although I didn't really want to, I went back. As a rule, I don't let strangers in my car. However, this woman looked desperate. While I debated what to do, I went inside the station's minimart and bought two bottles of mineral water from the cooler and secretly hoped she wouldn't be there when I got outside. She was.

I handed her a bottle of water. "Did you find a ride?" I asked.

"Yes, I did. I just called my sister, and she'll be here any minute." She paused, then touched my arm. "Thank you for the water."

About two seconds later her sister drove up. She got in the car, and they drove away. I didn't even catch her name.

Then I realized, her name was Jesus.

The woman and her two sons at the soup kitchen, Joe, Judy— they all were named Jesus.

When he was on earth, the Lord told his disciples, "For I was hungry and you gave me something to eat, I was thirsty and you gave me something to drink.... I tell you the truth, whatever you did for one of the least of these brothers of mine, you did for me" (Matthew 25:35,40).

I had opened my arms and extended my fingers to the poor and needy in more ways than I had envisioned; I had ministered not only to people but to Jesus.

When I got home, I raced to my desk, grabbed a pen, and crossed the "open arms" verse from my Proverbs 31 to-do list.

Then, flexing my fingers, I smiled.

Hands of Mercy

Any acts of mercy I have ever performed have been purely accidental. I don't have a merciful heart. My daughter Laura does, however.

A few years back, when a classmate of hers died after being hit by a car, she took all of her birthday money and gave it to the boy's family to help with funeral expenses. I doubt if she even thought about God rewarding her for it. (I would have.) She just did it out of a heart of mercy.

"Mercy is love reaching out to help those who are helpless and who need salvation," writes James Montgomery Boice in his commentary on the Sermon on the Mount. "Mercy identifies with the miserable in their misery."

I might be able to fake acts of charity—I can donate a can of green beans to the church food pantry and pretend I care—but true mercy can't be faked.

The Bible instructs us to "love mercy" (Micah 6:8). I can honestly say I love the mercy of God toward me—his reaching out to help me in my desperate need of salvation. But I can just as honestly say I don't love mercy the way God requires it of me.

That's a heart issue. It doesn't come naturally, at least not with me.

What does the Lord require of me? To act justly, to love mercy, and to walk humbly with him. The key is in the walking. The closer I draw to him in the walking, the more I'm overwhelmed by his boundless mercy and compassion for all who are needy, not just for me.

Soon my heart begins to soften. My arms start to extend to those around me. Then I find I don't just show mercy; I *love* mercy.

That's what God requires.

Digging Deeper

1. Using a dictionary and/or a thesaurus, define *mercy*. When was the last time someone extended mercy toward you? How did you feel? Would you have shown the same level of mercy if your roles had been reversed?

2. We can only show mercy to the extent that we've been shown mercy. What do the following passages say about the mercy of

God toward us: Matthew 20:29-34; Romans 9:15-24; 11:30-32; Ephesians 2:3-5; 1 Timothy 1:15-16; Titus 3:3-7?

3. Read 2 Samuel 9; Matthew 18:21-27; Luke 10:30-37. To whom and how is mercy extended in these passages?

4. Sometimes we become so caught up in our own daily trials that we forget to make time for the needs of others. Take some time today to meditate on Colossians 3:12. Who do you know that needs mercy? Make a list of ways you can pass God's mercy and compassion on to someone else this week.

"We do pray for mercy, and that same prayer doth teach us all to render the deeds of mercy."

—ANDREW MURRAY, as quoted in *God's Little Instruction Book on Prayer*

Chapter 12

Help, I'm Dyeing!

When it snows, she has no fear for her household;
for all of them are clothed in scarlet.

PROVERBS 31:21

We have a saying at our house: "It's better to be dead than caught wearing red." So you can imagine my distress at the thought of the next item on the VW to-do list: "When it snows, she has no fear for her household; for all of them are clothed in scarlet."

The snow portion of the verse didn't bother me—it doesn't snow in this part of Florida. However, the "dressed in scarlet" part caused me great mental anguish. So much so, that I considered giving up my Search for Virtue.

Let me explain. "Better dead than red" has not always been our family dictum. In fact, at one time we wore red as freely as the next family. Of course, that was before The Day I Dyed.

That morning began with one of my favorite pastimes, bleaching stuff in the washing machine. You know how kids ALWAYS say they won't spill grape juice? Well, I ALWAYS tell myself I won't spill bleach. Yeah, right. As always, I splashed bleach—on the sleeve of my new red shirt. Normally this might be cause for an "Oh drat!" or two, but for me it's an opportunity to indulge in another of my favorite pastimes: dyeing things.

Although according to my family, it's more like *killing* things, since I've yet to actually end up with anything wearable. Even so, there's something in me that quivers at the sight of a box of Rit dye. It's the same feeling I get when I see a Kevin Costner movie or discover I can still zip up my size-ten jeans.

Hello, my name is Nancy Kennedy, and I'm a dye-aholic.

At our previous houses, I had dyed all the time in a big washtub in the garage. However, we didn't bring my old washtub when we moved into that particular house. So I decided to do my dyeing in the bathtub. The easy, convenient, down-the-drain-when-finished bathtub.

A few minutes later I was sitting on the edge of my bathtub, watching it fill with steaming hot water and quivering in anticipation of dumping in the package of red fabric dye and swishing it around with my favorite wooden spoon.

But before I even got a chance to swish, red steam started to rise from the ceramic tub, forming red beads of sweat on the ceiling and trickling down the white painted wall in permanent, thin, red stripes. I grabbed the empty Rit box and read the instructions: DO NOT USE ON CERAMIC OR PAINTED SURFACES.

For a brief moment, caught up in a dye-induced high, I marveled at the artistry of it all—like a delicate watercolor painting. Except, of course, the "watercolor painting" was on my bathroom wall and not in a museum. The image of a less-than-delighted husband jarred me back to reality.

Common sense would say, "STOP NOW," but I couldn't bear the thought of a perfectly good tub of dye—or for that matter, a new shirt— going to waste. Besides, I hadn't gotten to swish yet. So, disregarding the mess, into the tub went my shirt—and along with it my wooden spoon. Again, common sense would say, "Forget the spoon. It's no big deal." Unfortunately, common sense has never been one of my strong points. Instead, I plunged my arms up to my elbows into the tub and felt around for the spoon.

"HOT tamales!" I yelled as I recoiled in pain, holding up two red arms like mercury rising inside two giant thermometers. Not only did the mercury rise, it also fell—all down my body and all over the floor.

I flicked a drip of red dye off the tip of my elbow, and it landed on my white sock.

At that point I could've—I should've—given up. But looking around the room, I realized I'd already gone too far to back out.

About that time, four-year-old Laura pushed the door open.

"Oh, Mommy!" she cried. "You're in BIG trouble!"

Startled, I spun around and, losing my balance, slipped on a puddle of red water, splattering the peach bath rug and the white-tiled floor, the white towels hanging on the towel bar, and the wallpaper behind them. The wallpaper I'd searched weeks to find. The wallpaper in the perfect peach and pale green plaid with coordinating tiny floral print border. MY wallpaper.

About the time things couldn't get much worse, our Labrador retriever came bounding up the stairs. "Samson, go outside!" I ordered.

He barged into the already-crowded bathroom and knocked Laura over with his tail. She landed with one white-sneakered foot in the tub.

"Samson!" she cried. "You're a dumb dog!"

Dumb is right. He leaped into the tubful of dye water and sat down for a bath.

"Get out, Samson!" I yelled, pulling on his chain. He wagged his tail, panted, lapped up some dye water, licked Laura's face, then shook. Shook red dye everywhere.

The clothes I was wearing—my favorite pink shorts and aqua T-shirt—now were red polka-dotted. The sink was red polka-dotted. The mirror was red polka-dotted. Laura and I were red polka-dotted.

Samson was half blond, half red.

I took off Laura's polka-dotted clothes, toweled her off, and sent her to her room to change.

"What are we going to do with you?" I asked Samson as I scooped red dog hair out of the tub. He wagged his tail and gave another shake.

I looked around the bathroom, shrugged my shoulders, and laughed to keep myself from crying. "I might as well dye everything!" I said in my dyeing stupor, then peeled off my shorts, T-shirt, sneakers, and socks, and tossed them in the tub with Samson. I threw all the towels, the bath rug, and Laura's other white shoe in too, then sat down on the edge of the tub.

"What do we do now, Samson?" I asked. He slurped red dye on my face.

So there I sat: two red arms, one red cheek, a dog with a wagging red tail, assorted red splotches everywhere, wearing just my red polka-dotted bra and underwear.

Of course, the phone rang.

"Laura!" I called through clenched, polka-dotted teeth. "Get the phone. Tell whoever it is I'm BUSY!"

"Oh, Grandma!" I heard Laura wail. "Mommy can't come to the phone right now. She's upstairs, dyeing in the bathroom!"

Within minutes, my mom burst through the bathroom door, certain she'd find her firstborn lying in a pool of blood. At least she got the pool part right.

"Hi, Mom. What's new?" I asked from the bathroom floor.

She didn't answer. She just stared.

Although the full weight of my predicament hadn't hit me, I had a hunch I was in trouble. "Mom, I think I've got Cats in the Hats."

Now in case you aren't aware, Cats in the Hats—at least according to my mom—are what you get when one mess leads to another, like in the Dr. Seuss book *The Cat in the Hat Comes Back*. The Cat eats pink cake in the bathtub, wipes the pink tub ring with Mother's white dress, wipes the dress on the wall, then on Dad's ten-dollar shoes, the rug, and Dad's bed.

Eventually the pink mess ends up in the snow, and only a tiny creature called a VOOM can clean it up.

"Mom, say something!"

She did. She repeated, "Oh, Nancy," about twenty times. At the twenty-first "Oh, Nancy," she added a sigh and a "Thank you for not doing this at my house." After mumbling a few more "Oh, Nancy's," Mom picked up her car keys and turned to go.

"Don't leave me!" I cried.

"Don't worry. I'll be back," she said, and taking Laura with her, she left me alone with my Cats in the Hats. And my red dog. While Mom was gone, I managed to drain the tub and get Samson out without creating more C in the Hs. (I put newspapers down everywhere and covered him up with a blanket until he made it out the back door.)

Mom returned a short time later—with a VOOM. Only her VOOM came in the form of a few bowling league friends toting buckets and sponges.

Thank God for mothers. They always seem to know what to do in an emergency.

We mopped and scrubbed and did what we could. One woman scoured the tub; another went outside and scoured the dog.

Mom scoured me.

At the end of the day, she and her friends packed up their buckets and left. The walls still needed repapering and repainting, and the tub needed reglazing, but that would have to wait for another day.

When Barry walked in at 5:30, he found Laura and me curled up on the couch, reading a book. "Hi, guys," he said. "Anything interesting happen today?"

"Well, I started a redecorating project," I told him.

"That's nice," he said and went into the bathroom to take a shower.

I don't really want to go into the rest of the story. Let's just say I ended up having to promise no more dyeing ever, and I had to help pay for the repairs. Also, Barry banned the color red permanently from our house.

"That's why I can't ever fulfill this verse," I moaned as I recalled my Last Dyeing Day.

Could I?

After much thought, I went ahead and marked it off as a Virtuous experience. Mess and damage notwithstanding, technically I'd done what I thought the verse required. After all, I did dye everything scarlet, didn't I?

How Firm a Foundation

What can I say? It's a gift: If it can make a mess, wreak havoc, or cause a catastrophe, I'll step in it. Take the time my husband and I went up into the attic to run a cable line. My job was to hold the flashlight and *stay on the rafters*. Instead, I found myself up to my thigh, dangling through a hole in the Sheetrock. I had stepped off the rafters—a firm foundation—and into trouble.

Many times I cause my own troubles, but many times trouble just happens. Life is full of trouble and trials: financial setbacks, illness, relationship woes. Jesus warned us so we wouldn't be surprised. But he also said we shouldn't let our hearts be troubled or afraid. Instead, he said to trust in God and also in him (John 14:1). He also told a story about foundations and the importance of having one that's strong and steady and sure. He said a foolish man builds a house on sand, but a wise one builds on rock. When the storms come, the beachfront house washes away, but the one on rock remains steadfast.

The rock is the Word and character of God. If that's our foundation, if that's our standard and rule for our lives, when trouble comes, our lives won't crumble or crash around us.

The Proverbs Thirty-One Woman didn't fear winter, or seasons of trouble, because she was prepared. Her foundation was sure. Likewise, when my foundation is God himself and I stand firmly upon his Word, I, too, don't need to be afraid when trouble comes. I only need to fear when I step off.

Digging Deeper

1. Someone once said, "In adversity we usually want God to do a removing job when he wants to do an improving job. To realize the worth of the anchor, we need to feel the storm." When was the last time you were in a storm of trouble? Describe your response and what you learned about God and yourself.

2. In the following scriptures, what does the Bible say about trials, storms, and trouble? Psalms 9:9; 34; 37:39; 46; 86:6-7; John 16:33; 2 Corinthians 4:17; James 1:2-4,12; 5:13; 1 Peter 4:12-16. How can these verses prepare us for trouble? This week make an effort to memorize one or more of these scriptures.

3. Read the parable of the wise and the foolish builders in Matthew 7:24-27. Rewrite or retell it in modern terms. How do people today "build on sand"?

4. Using a concordance, look up the word *rock* as it pertains to God. How is God a rock in your life during times of trouble?

"The reason why the Bible spends so much of its time reiterating that God is a strong rock, a firm defense, and a sure refuge and help for the weak is that God spends so much of his time showing us that we are weak, both mentally and morally, and dare not trust ourselves to find or follow the right road."

—JAMES PACKER, *Your Father Loves You*

Chapter 13

Can't Help Lovin' That Man of Mine

She makes coverings for her bed.
PROVERBS 31:22

Dear Mrs. P.,

Did this ever happen to you? It seems that after nearly twenty years of marriage, things cool down a bit, if you know what I mean. Where it used to be evenings of dancing by firelight to Johnny Mathis songs and passionate kisses before breakfast, it's now side-by-side toenail clipping by the light of the evening news and a morning pat on the head as we pass in the hallway.

Oh sure, we still have moments of passion—like when there's only one Snickers bar left in the cupboard and we arm-wrestle each other for it. Or the times my husband pulls the covers down because he's hot, and I yank them back up because I'm cold. Or when we play the Thermostat Game where one person turns it up to a reasonable, comfortable temperature and the other one plunges the house into a sub-zero state of hypothermia.

But you probably want to know about you-know-what. You-know-what is fine, thank you. Except, well, after nineteen years, it has lost some of its…you know. It's like white bread and vanilla pudding. You know exactly what you're getting, and you're never disappointed, but you're never surprised either.

Did you and Mr. P. experience this too?

I find it troubling. That's why I decided we needed a little excitement in our you-know-what life.

I bought a book.

According to *Steps to Better You-Know-What,* first I needed to take inventory of our bedroom, which could only be described as Slovenly Functional. The dresser served as a catchall for peach pits and apple cores, magazines and who knows what else.

The bedspread, once a pristine, cream-colored eyelet, had seen one too many spilled bowls of chocolate ice cream over the years. (Did Mr. P. drip ice cream too? Is that why you made coverings for your bed?)

Our boudoir needed a boost. I cleaned everything off the dresser, polished the wood until it glowed, set out baskets of dried flowers, dusted months' worth of cobwebs, and replaced the old bedspread with a new patchwork quilt.

Next thing the book said was to Notice Your Man. "Notice his muscular legs, masculine chest, broad shoulders, and all of his other manly traits."

I marched into the living room where Barry sat intently watching the hockey game. With notebook in hand, I circled him, Noticing Him and making notes. When I'd gathered enough notes, I turned off the TV and said, "Nice eyes."

The book said he'd respond with chest-puffing and smiling, but obviously Barry hadn't read the book. He responded by flipping the TV back on and asking me to please get out of the way.

I tried again. "Hubba hubba, love those legs."

Barry lifted his head for a microsecond, long enough to reply, "Hubba hubba, what is your problem?" then went right back to following the puck on the ice.

"I'm just Noticing My Man, that's all."

"Well, can you notice me some other time? I'm trying to watch the game."

Well, Mrs. P., that didn't work. Luckily, *Steps* is a big book and contains lots more suggestions. The next chapter recommended "Tell Your Man You Love Him Just the Way He Is." The following night I waited until the hockey game was almost over before I made my move. I put on my cardigan sweater and changed into tennis shoes and in my best Mr. Rogers voice said, "Barry, there's only one you—and I like you just the way you are."

He suggested I take a ride on the trolley.

The next night I read: "Compare him to a famous masculine character." This time I waited until the hockey game went into overtime before I even set foot in the living room.

"Did I ever tell you how much you remind me of Fred Flintstone?" I said to my cave man in the blue armchair. "And when you had that stomach virus last week and your face was all green and contorted, you looked just like the Incredible Hulk."

He waited until the commercial to respond. "What's going on with you?" he asked. "You've been acting weird all week, and now you're insulting me. Are you mad at me?"

I showed him a magazine quiz I'd taken just that morning, "How's the Zip in Your Zip-A-Dee-Do-Dah?" As a couple, we'd rated a twenty-four out of a possible one hundred. "Barry, according to this quiz, since we don't take moonlit walks and serenade each other over the phone, we're duds in the romance department. We don't even have an 'our song.'"

His face said, "Oh brother," but his mouth said, "If you're unhappy, then we can talk about it. Later. After the hockey game."

"I'm not unhappy," I told him. "In fact, everything's fine. But, well, you know. Things could be better. Anyway, that's what the book says." I started to show him *Steps* but thought better of it. It's best to leave a few surprises in your marriage (*Steps,* page 173). Besides, the hockey game was back on, and Barry hinted that I might prefer reading in another room.

I opened to the chapter on "Setting the Stage for Love." It suggested I create "An Evening in Spain" by meeting Barry at the door wearing a mantilla in my hair and a rose in my teeth.

The next night I put on some flamenco music, and as he walked in the door, I started to shout *"Olé!"* to surprise him, but instead it came out "O-yeow!" because my lips got caught on the thorny rose stem. My mantilla fell off, and the Paella Helper burned. I spent the rest of the night with an ice cube on my lip, reading my book.

Mrs. P., the more I read, the more I suspected nothing it suggested was going to work. Not calling him "my Hunky Punky," not putting muskrat oil on my pulse points, not even singing, "It's So Nice to Have a Man Around the House."

The next night I gave up. Actually, I gave in. I'd spent the day reading what the Bible had to say about a wife's role in marriage, and I discovered I'd been going about this all wrong. First Corinthians 11:9 says woman was created for man. That tells me I'm to fit in with Barry's plans, submit myself to him, adapt myself to him, speak his own romantic language— and quit trying to run the show my way. Even when it comes to you-know-what.

So I simply threw the book in the trash, put on Barry's old hockey jersey, and splashed on some Eau de Zamboni (that's a perfume that smells like skate leather and sweaty Frenchmen). Then I flopped down on the couch next to him to watch that night's hockey game.

Well, Mrs. P., you'll never guess what happened next. Just as I got interested in the game, Barry began edging closer. "Mmmm, come here and give me a kiss," he said, nuzzling my neck.

"But, Barry, the game's on," I said.

"Who cares about the game?" He shut off the TV—during the last five minutes of the third period with the score tied—and pulled me to my feet.

"Barry, all week I've been knocking myself out trying to get your attention and improve our you-know-what, and this is what sparks your interest?"

He didn't answer. I didn't answer. We... Well, normally I'd tell you the rest of the story, but this time, well, you know.

Have to go now. Give my regards to Mr. P. and all your household.

Sincerely,

Nancy Kennedy

Complete, Not Compete

It's the struggle of the ages: God created the woman to be a "suitable helper" to the man, and ever since, the woman has tried to reverse it. We might not say it out loud, but something in us rises up and says, "No man's going to tell *me* what to do!"

While the Lord never intended the man to rule over his wife with an iron fist—the Bible teaches mutual submission—he did say the man is to be the leader in his family. A woman is to be his complement. She's to be a gracious responder, adapting herself to his leading. Not as a doormat or begrudgingly, but "as is fitting in the Lord" (Colossians 3:18).

God designed men with a need to be needed, as protectors, providers, leaders, lovers. In *What Makes a Man Feel Loved*, Bob Barnes writes, "One way to melt a man's heart is to show him that you truly need him. The simple, direct statement, 'I need your help' reinforces your husband's masculinity. Most husbands won't refuse a wife's straightforward expression of a need."

Most men take pleasure and derive great satisfaction in their role as provider and leader, and a wife who encourages her husband in those responsibilities does them both a favor. Barnes says, when you allow a man to act from his sense of masculinity, you'll probably also find yourself feeling closer to him because he has just taken care of you in some way.

You could say being a complement is a way to give your husband a compliment.

Digging Deeper

1. What do you think it means to be submissive? What are some of the misconceptions people have about this word?

2. God designed women to be responders. In a graceful waltz, a man leads and a woman follows. In sexual intimacy, the wife responds to her husband's leading. In what other ways can wives be responders to their husbands? How do some women resist this role?

3. Read what the Bible says about submission, beginning with the example of Jesus in Philippians 2:1-16. See also Ephesians 5:21-24; Colossians 3:15-18; James 4:6-8; and 1 Peter 3:1-6. What are the elements of true biblical submission? How does this differ from your answer to the first question?

4. The Bible instructs wives to adapt or fit in with their husbands' plans and holds up Sarah as an example (1 Peter 3:5-6). As you read about her in Genesis 12 and Genesis 16–21, note the ways she adapted to her husband's plans. What can we learn from her? Are there limits to submission? Acts 5:29 gives the definitive guideline: "We must obey God rather than men!" That's where a knowledge of Scripture enters in. We must know what God says in order to know our limits. What are some instances when refusing to submit would be the right thing to do?

"Submissiveness is a matter not of mere outward form but of inner attitude. A wife can be a person of strong opinions and still be submissive to her husband's authority if deep down she respects him and is quite prepared and content for him to make and carry out the final decision. On the other hand, a wife who scarcely opens her mouth with an idea of her own and never questions her husband's decisions may, underneath it all, nurse a deep, sullen rebellion."

—LARRY CHRISTENSON, *The Christian Family*

Chapter 14

Does an Outfit of Strength and Dignity Come in Pink?

She is clothed in fine linen and purple.

PROVERBS 31:22

She is clothed with strength and dignity.

PROVERBS 31:25

While the VW wears the haute couture of fine linen and purple, the truth is, I don't know how to dress. I mean, sure, I buy a lot of clothes, and I can put on my pants and button my shirt. But chances are, the combination of the two won't get me on the cover of *Vogue*. As for being clothed with strength and dignity, I secretly hoped that meant jeans and a T-shirt.

One morning as I stared into my jam-packed closet, I realized I had nothing to wear to an upcoming lunch meeting with a new editor, so I called a friend for advice.

"Maria, I need you to help me pick out something strong and dignified," I pleaded. "Or at least something I can still fit into that will be somewhat presentable."

She came right over and joined me in staring into the closet. "Nancy," she said as she held out outfit after outfit, "no offense, but…" She didn't finish her sentence; she just shook her head.

I don't know about you, but I know I'm in trouble when someone starts off a sentence, "No offense, but…" as in, "No offense, but that outfit you're wearing looks like something Ronald McDonald once rejected."

She stepped back and tossed up her hands. "The problem is, you have a lot of stuff here, but you can't wear any of it to your meeting."

She started pitching my favorite outfits into one huge reject pile: my "If I Only Had a Brain" sweatshirt, my neon pink turtleneck and matching bolero pants, even my faux fur-collared, brown imitation-vinyl ski jacket. She tossed until there was nothing left.

"Anything else wrong with my clothes?" I asked, watching one lone coat hanger wobble on the bar.

"Nope, that about does it."

We sat together on the closet floor and picked at carpet lint as she broached the subject of my need for what she called "a total wardrobal revision."

"Nancy," she said, only it sounded more like "Naaan-ceeeee," which usually means I'm about to get lectured about something I'm doing wrong. My mother called me Naaan-ceeeee whenever she found ancient pizza boxes under the couch or a red sock mixed in with the wet, white laundry.

"Naaan-ceeeee, didn't anyone tell you that you can't wear peach?"

I looked over at the pile of clothes on the floor, half of them peach. "Why can't I?"

"Because, my friend, you're obviously a 'Summer,' and Summers don't wear peach. It makes them look like the third day of a five-day virus. Haven't you ever noticed people covering their faces whenever you wear peach?"

"Fine," I said, "so I look sick when I wear peach. Can I wear taupe?"

"Uh-uh."

"Cream or beige?"

She made a gagging gesture that I took to mean no.

"What's left?" I asked.

"Light pink and any shade of blue."

"I'll feel like a maternity ward," I said, picturing blue booties and pink sunbonnets. I picked up a lemon-yellow blouse and held it up to my face. "Maria, are you sure?"

"Trust me."

The last time a friend said that, I ended up on the back of a wayward horse who didn't understand that "Whoa!" means "Stop" or that tree branches don't yield the right of way—and I've got the scar on my leg to prove it. But since Maria didn't mention horses, I agreed to trust her with my lack of haute or any other kind of couture and followed my friend's lead to the mall.

Now, back before shopping became a science, I liked going to the mall. I could people-watch, get some exercise walking around, and most important, buy anything in any color I wanted. But that day, with Maria calling cadence while I marched ten steps behind, it felt more like a military mission than something fun.

She led me over to a bench and pulled out her battle plans. "First we'll storm Macy's, then torpedo the smaller shops, and finally we'll blast our way through the shoe and accessory stores."

She called our mission "Dress to Impress," our motto being, "If it doesn't scream Power, put it back."

According to Maria's battle plans, I needed a Power Outfit for my upcoming meeting. By that she meant a suit. I, on the other hand, was hoping for a new pair of jeans and maybe a pink sweater.

One of the benefits of being a writer is that you aren't seen by anyone except the mailman and the meter reader. You can safely sit at your computer in yesterday's T-shirt with the ketchup stain on the sleeve and mismatched socks and still maintain the illusion of being a Put Together Businesswoman. To me, new jeans and a pink sweater are formalwear compared to my usual attire.

"Dress to Impress," Maria reminded me as I tried on suit after suit. We looked for something simple and conservative—feminine but not froufrou—finally deciding on a straight navy blue skirt and a pink jacket with navy windowpane lines. Maria deemed it perfect. I thought it made me look like a kid playing dress up with her mom's clothes, but at least it was linen and fulfilled that point of the verse.

"Trust me, we're not finished," assured General Maria as she handed me the rest of my outfit over the dressing room door.

As per Maria's command, underneath the jacket went a white silk blouse; underneath that went a camisole; underneath that went a pair of shoulder pads. Because I've had a couple of kids and still have what my husband affectionately refers to as "abdominal overhang" (or as I overheard my doctor tell his tape recorder, "excess adipose tissue"), Maria shoved me into some stomach-restricting foundations. I couldn't breathe and sit at the same time, but at least I could button my jacket.

Next my outfit needed shoes—high heels. I'll spare you my feelings on those. Let's just say I know they were designed by a podiatrist who needed some extra business. However, Maria assured me they were nonnegotiable. "You can't show up wearing your Reeboks or those horrible open-toed brown things of yours," she warned me.

After the shoes and matching clutch bag ("Nancy, kiss that duffel bag you call a purse good-bye"), we completed my $423.57 outfit with a faux gold chain, a pair of (again, faux) gold earrings, and (in my opinion) a stupid-looking scarf to hang over my left shoulder. I just spent my entire year's clothing budget on one Power Outfit that made me feel foolish, squashed my stomach, and pinched my toes. I guess that's what power does to a person.

On the morning of my big lunch, Maria came over to supervise my dressing, just in case I decided to dig something out of the reject pile.

With my battle gear in place, I have to admit, power surged through my pink-jacketed body. I was going to march into that restaurant, Dressed to Impress—stupid-looking scarf and all—and bowl that editor over with my presence.

March I did, right out of the car and into a puddle. I wobbled into the restaurant (I told you, I'd never worn heels before) and into the ladies' room to wash off my stockings and shoes. In the process I got the stupid-looking scarf wet, and the colors (navy, pink, and turquoise) bled onto my jacket.

I thought I could get away with removing my jacket and wearing just the skirt and blouse, but that's when I discovered silk makes me sweat. And since wearing sweaty white silk is a lot like wearing nothing at all, I had no choice but to keep my jacket on and stay turned to the right.

Already ten minutes late, I wobbled and squished into the restaurant to meet the woman who held my writing future in her hands. I took a step toward her and, in an attempt to stay turned to the right, got my heel caught on the edge of my chair and fell off my shoes, landing sprawled at her feet.

It's true—your whole life passes before your eyes when you're dying, and dying of embarrassment is no exception. At that moment, a career in sewage treatment didn't sound half bad.

I know I was on the floor for only a few seconds, but it seemed like hours. As I lay there, I considered slinking away, unnoticed. However, it was too late for that—people generally notice other people prostrating themselves on a restaurant floor.

I'll fake an injury. Then everyone will feel sorry for me, and I can salvage my dignity.

My dignity! The VW wore dignity, as well as strength. Of course, she probably didn't let her friend talk her into wearing a Power Outfit. She wore fine linen and purple because of who she was, not because of who she wanted to impress. Her power came from her character. And if I wanted to be like Madame VW, I'd have to draw my power from the same source.

From my vantage point on the floor, I saw I had two choices: I could get up and run out of there, never show my face in public again (especially at that restaurant), plus give up my writing career. Or I could get up, introduce myself, and laugh it off.

Either way, I had to get up.

"A simple curtsy will do," the editor said, helping me to my feet. She grinned, and for a moment, I sensed everything would be all right. That is, until I discovered shoulder pads shift during a free fall.

I took a breath, then smiled as if this were an everyday occurrence. "How do you do," I said, holding out one hand and trying to retrieve the wayward foam rubber pads with the other. "I'm Nancy Kennedy, the world's only three-breasted hunchback."

Once we were both seated and I'd shifted to the right, she leaned forward. "You won't believe the lengths people go through to try to impress me. It's refreshing to see you're secure enough not to fall into that trap."

I just smiled and tugged at my skirt as it rode up my knees. We were halfway through our Caesar salads when I realized I hadn't even taken note of my lunch companion's outfit. That's when I noticed her neon pink turtleneck. I covered my mouth to conceal a smile.

I peeked under the tablecloth. Another concealed smile: matching bolero pants. I looked again and this time didn't hide my delight: open-toed brown shoes.

Now that's what I call a Power Outfit.

Wearing the Right Clothes

From the time they could say, "Oh, *gross!*" my daughters have been trying to give me a fashion makeover. They hate my black floral jumper and call the vests I like to wear "hideous." They refuse to be seen with me when I'm wearing…just about anything I own. They especially hate my skirted bathing suits, but as I've informed them, when you have a forty-year-old derriere, you *need* to skirt the issue.

Recently at one daughter's insistence I bought some capri pants. I actually liked them and so did my daughter. She said they make me look "almost cool."

Trouble was, I had to buy a shirt to go with it. Then I had to buy the right kind of shoes. Then I needed a haircut. That led to needing the right kind of earrings and the right kind of nail polish.

All for a pair of capri pants that will go out of style before I wear them twice.

The Proverbs Thirty-One Woman always wore the right outfit. The passage says she is clothed in "fine linen and purple" (verse 22) as well as with "strength and dignity" (verse 25). In those days, fine linen was worn by priests, and purple signified royalty.

She was a daughter of the King, the Lord Almighty, a priestess to her family, with a character of strength and dignity. That's the outfit she wore every day, and because I, too, am a daughter of the King, that's my daily attire as well.

As Christians, we have been given Christ's robe of righteousness. We wear his virtue and his goodness, his strength and his dignity. Capri pants may come and go, but an outfit such as that will never go out of style.

Digging Deeper

1. What is the one outfit or item in your closet that you absolutely love to wear? Why?

2. As Christians, we all have one particular garment in common: a robe of righteousness. Look up the following scriptures, and in your own words write out how a person can obtain this garment: Zechariah 3:3-4; Matthew 22:1-14; Isaiah 61:10.

3. Along with our robe of righteousness, we are told to clothe ourselves with certain virtues. Read the following verses and note each virtue listed, then use a dictionary or a thesaurus to capture the full meaning: Colossians 3:12-14; 1 Peter 5:5-6.

Other scriptures tell us to "put off" some things and "put on" others. Read through the following verses, then list and define these characteristics as well: Romans 13:12-14; Ephesians 4:22-32; Colossians 3:9-10.

4. Christians have been given one more outfit, found in Ephesians 6:10-18. List and describe each part of this outfit. What does each item of this wardrobe do for a Christian? Have you been neglecting any particular piece of your spiritual clothing? Ask God to help you as you "get dressed" every morning.

~

"Dressed in his righteousness alone, faultless to stand before the throne."

—WILLIAM B. BRADBURY, "The Solid Rock"

Chapter 15

From Rags to...Rags

Her husband is respected at the city gate.
PROVERBS 31:23

I've come to a conclusion: Men wear frayed, bleached out, torn-armpitted, and knee-holed clothing on purpose. I'm not sure, but I think it has something to do with testosterone. Have you ever seen a woman wearing a Super Bowl XVI T-shirt with one sleeve missing and the neck binding torn off, ambiguously colored gym shorts, grayed socks with heel holes, or the remains of a ten-year-old pair of canvas deck shoes? I didn't think so. It's gotta be a guy thing.

I did some research on the subject recently while hanging around the plumbing supply aisle at the hardware store, waiting for my husband to select a T-joint something or other. I noticed that out of a dozen men milling around looking at pipe dope and plumbing stuff, none wore shoes without holes and dirty, broken laces; T-shirts without a frayed neck binding, torn pocket, or splashes of that morning's coffee; or jeans that didn't expose entire kneecaps. Not only that, half of them needed a shave, and someone needed a shower, although I couldn't tell who.

I found the whole thing fascinating, but I couldn't very well go up to one of them and ask, "Excuse me, but can you tell me why you seem oblivious to the fact that you look like someone mopped the floor with you?" I couldn't even ask Barry, since he was one of them in his paint-splattered, one-and-a-half-sleeved, once-white T-shirt and shredded shorts.

I mean, do guys get up every morning and say to themselves, "What is the ugliest, rattiest, dirtiest dust rag with arm and leg holes that I can wear in public?" Do they deliberately go to the laundry basket and pull out whatever's on the bottom? Or is it an unconscious thing?

This poses a problem to potential VWs of today. I once heard a radio pastor explain Proverbs 31:23 this way: "The Virtuous Woman's husband is respected at the city gate because of his clean appearance and neat clothing. Everything about him is decent and handsome, yet not gaudy. Everyone knows he has a proper wife at home who takes care of him."

I gulped when I heard that. I gulped and squirmed and let out a tiny whimper. *If that's true,* I thought, *then my husband's appearance is a reflection on me.*

And so, with the most noble of intentions (that of making myself look like a good wife), I set out to change the situation right then and there. "My husband WILL be respected at the city gate," I said as I plotted my major husbandly wardrobe overhaul. "Barry's going to be respected—whether he likes it or not."

The next day, as a spider would ensnare a fly, I lured Barry to the mall with the promise of a major appliance sale at Sears. Once I caught him in my web, he was all mine.

"Look over here," I said as I dragged him over to the men's department, despite his desperate attempts to plant the heels of his grass-stained Reeboks in front of a forty-gallon water heater. "Let's pick out some shirts."

"I have shirts," he answered. "What I want is an air compressor."

"Barry, what you have are exposed armpits and chest hair. Those things you call shirts look as if someone attacked them with a cheese grater."

"So?"

"So! So you need to pick out some shirts."

You know the way cranky toddlers toss back their heads and wail, "Do

I have to?" Well, picture one with a five o'clock shadow and hairier arms, and you have a picture of my husband standing in front of the polo shirt rack.

We (I) picked out a black one, a purple one, and one of turquoise blue, while he tapped his foot on the floor and made faces in the three-way mirror. Next we (I) picked out a few pairs of Dockers slacks, and I tapped my foot until he went in the dressing room and tried them on. Honestly, you'd have thought I'd asked him to give up a kidney.

After that, we (I) moved over to the shoe department; then I went back and moved Barry there too. "Shoes," I said. "You need shoes."

"What's wrong with these?" "These" being sneakers worn to play basketball, spread weed-and-feed on a muddy lawn, stain a patio deck, and engage in various and sundry other activities, each of which had left an indelible mark.

"To put it bluntly, they're disgusting, and you can't wear them anymore," I said, handing him the checkbook.

His head flew back again, toddler-style. "Don't wanna," he said. "Can't we just go home?"

"Can't you just write out the check?" I pleaded, then quickly changed my tactic. "You know, Barry, you look awfully cute in your new clothes," I said in my sweetest spoonful-of-sugar voice. "Maybe when we get home..." (I whispered the rest in his ear.)

He smiled and wrote the check as fast as he could. (The promise of sauerkraut chili dogs gets him every time.)

Upon returning home, he immediately tossed his shopping bags into the closet and raced toward the kitchen while I stood, mouth agape. "Barry!" I called. "You're doing it all wrong!"

He appeared in the doorway with a package of hot dogs in his hands. "What are you talking about? I know how to cook hot dogs."

Poor man, he obviously didn't know the *après* shopping routine. "I'm not talking about hot dogs; I'm talking about shopping. First you throw out all your old stuff, then you spread your new stuff out on the bed. Next you list how many outfits you can make out of your purchases and whatever might be left in the closet."

After I explained the procedure, he gave me the Guy Version: Throw the bags in the closet and forget all about them, then go about your business wearing the same old stuff you've been wearing all along, except maybe add a new baseball hat. Then, after about seven years, take the clothes out of the bags and let them sit on top of the dresser for a few months. After that, wash everything about fifteen times. As for new shoes, wear them when cleaning the chimney or varnishing a boat. Only then are a guy's clothes suitable for public wear.

We took our discussion into the kitchen and volleyed fashion maxims around for a while until it escalated into a fight.

"You're just trying to change me," Barry accused.

"No, I'm not. I just think you'll be happier if you did things the right way and if you wore clothes that actually had fibers holding them together—and in recognizable colors."

We stood nose to chest (he's a foot taller than I am) as we did the "If you loved me, you'd _____" routine until we ended up with no solution, only singed hot dogs. He insisted on maintaining the status quo (wearing his same comfortable rags) while I held out for nothing less than his being the next *GQ* cover model.

Now do you see how hard it is to obtain Virtue in true Proverbs 31 tradition? I ask you, how can my husband be respected at the city gate unless he tosses his rags and wears real clothes so all the people will see (and therefore think he's got a proper wife at home)?

Obviously, shopping wasn't enough. We'd reached a crisis point, and I needed to bring out the big guns. When Barry went off to work the next day, I did a little closet updating on my own. Out went the rust-colored corduroy jeans with the shiny seat. Out went the sweatpants with the missing drawstring. Out went the Baltimore Colts jersey and the grayed underwear and the socks with toe holes.

Basically, out went everything.

By the time Barry came home, I'd replaced every ragged, ratty piece of clothing with something new, clean, and fresh. Not to mention respectable.

While not exactly expecting accolades, I at least hoped he'd see the error of his stubborn ways and give me a token "You're right. I was wrong." Instead, I got grunts. And whimpers. And moans.

"I have nothing to wear!" he cried as he leafed through the rows of neatly hung shirts and slacks in his closet. "What did you do with my clothes?"

I pointed to three Hefty garbage bags sitting out on the curb for the next morning's trash pickup. For what happened next, I can again only blame testosterone. He ran out to the curb, tore open the bags, and caressed the contents. For a moment I was jealous—I couldn't remember the last time he'd shown me that much affection.

I was totally confused. "Barry, how can you expect to be respected at the city gate—or even at the local Dunkin' Donuts—if you insist on wearing rags?"

"Look, I don't know where you get these ideas, but my reputation is just fine. Nancy, you're a good woman: You work hard, you keep the kids happy and well-behaved, plus you do all sorts of little things for me like packing my lunch every day. That's what people notice. And my friends respect me because of those things. As for my clothes, I don't have to dress to impress anybody but myself." He cradled his eighth-grade Westbury Junior High gym shorts. "Besides, here's how I see it: When you and the girls are dressed nice, *that* makes me look good."

There in a nutshell was the essence of the Respected at the City Gate verse, according to Barry Kennedy.

Well then, if my being dressed nicely makes him look good, who am I to argue? After all, my goal is to have my husband respected at the city gate, and if that means going out and buying myself all new clothes, that's just a sacrifice I'll have to make.

I'm excited to tell you, I crossed verse 23 off my list the other day after I hit a huge clearance sale down at the mall. Of course, Barry still wears his frayed jeans and holey T-shirts down at the city gate, but with me wearing all my new outfits, he looks *great*.

Lookin' Good

Want to know the best way to make a man look good? Give him an encouraging wife. He'll walk a little straighter, sit a bit taller, smile more easily.

What does encouragement look like? In a survey of several hundred men across the nation, marriage and family counselor H. Norman Wright asked, "What one thing would you like your wife to do that would (encourage) you in your daily life?"

Some of their answers include:

- Be a sounding board without judging.
- Show genuine interest in my work.
- Give me space to unwind when I first come home.
- Acknowledge that I'm doing the best I can, even if I don't measure up to your desires or expectations.
- Don't compare me to other husbands or fathers.
- Accept that we're different.
- Don't put my interests down.
- Accept me for who I am. Don't push me into being something I'm not. Have patience with me—help me be a better me, not a different me.

One man answered, "The one thing I would like my wife to do is to encourage me. To create for me a place in her arms or in my home that is a shelter from the things I'm dealing with, not more demands or expectations." Another said, "Tell me things like 'You're doing so well,' 'You can do it,' and 'I know what you do will be the best.' Respect me and be thankful for how I provide. Accept my choices and decisions without criticism, challenge, or smart remarks. I want to know my wife is on my side."

When a man's wife is on his side, he'll wear her honor and respect when he's out at the "city gates"—and it will wear well.

Digging Deeper

1. We all know women who tear their husbands down and even berate them in public. What do you think happens to these men (and these marriages) when this behavior becomes a regular pattern? How do others view the men? their wives? Now think back on your recent conversations about your husband. In what ways might your comments have increased or decreased others' respect for him?

2. Ephesians 5:33 in *The Amplified Bible* says, "Let the wife see that she **respects** and **reverences** her husband [that she **notices** him, **regards** him, **honors** him, **prefers** him, **venerates**, and **esteems** him; and that she **defers** to him, **praises** him, and **loves** and **admires** him exceedingly]." Create a list of the words set in bold type, then use a dictionary or a thesaurus to look up the definition of each. Beside each word, list some ways wives can show their husbands respect. How might a woman's respect effect change in her husband?

3. All Christians are called to be encouragers. Read the following verses, then describe how these truths can help you find ways to encourage your husband: Matthew 7:1-5; Ephesians 4:25–5:2; Philippians 4:8; Titus 2:4-5; Philemon 7.

4. If you're married, write a letter to your husband telling him what you admire about him. Be specific and generous with your admiration. One of the best ways a wife can encourage her husband is by praying for him. Ask how you can pray for him. Just your asking will be a great encouragement to him.

"The law of admiration…is the basis of all lasting, growing relationships. The vital part is that you don't have to like a person to admire him or her. Admiring someone is a choice, a decision, a commitment, an act of our will. It's telling ourselves, 'God loves and values that person, and so can I.'"

—GARY SMALLEY, *For Better or for Best*

Chapter 16

Attack of the *PDS Monster

*Patty Duke Syndrome

She makes linen garments and sells them.

PROVERBS 31:24

Why is it that so many women, once reasonably sane, at some point in their lives become overwhelmed with the need to dress themselves and their female offspring in matching attire? I call it the Patty Duke Syndrome ("They laugh alike, they walk alike, at times they even talk alike. You could lose your mind…"). I have no substantiating documentation to back me up, but I'm guessing that even the multitalented VW of Proverbs 31 suffered from PDS.

I remember when it struck my mom. (So young too.) She sat at her sewing machine for weeks making matching Easter dresses for herself, my sister, Peggy, and me. I can still see them: custard yellow, sleeveless, collarless, button-down-the-back-and-tie-dresses that were so popular in the early sixties, with yellow-and-white striped skirts and yellow patch pockets. If I recall correctly, we looked adorable, like three pats of butter with bare arms and legs.

Unfortunately, it didn't stop there. I think because of the adorability factor, my mother decided that, if one outfit reaches an eight on the "aren't they cute" scale, just think what twelve would reach!

Mom, bless her PDS-afflicted heart, set out to turn us into the Stepford Trio. As far as we were concerned, the Easter dresses were okay, because Peggy and I were still young and didn't know any better. But as we grew up, matching gingham cowgirl dresses with red felt hats and red bandannas didn't exactly get the kinds of looks from boys that we might have wanted. We felt like geeks extraordinaire.

One Christmas she dressed us up in red-and-white striped pantsuits with green sashes and red Santa hats on our heads. For Valentine Day we wore red baby-doll dresses, white tights, and black patent-leather shoes. And those Pilgrim outfits we wore one Thanksgiving… Well, let's just say they made Peggy and me feel like turkeys.

I'll never forget the summer we took a boat to Catalina, a small island off the California coast. Mom surprised us by unpacking our suitcases before we left home and replacing our meticulously chosen outfits with— you guessed it. That summer marked Mom's Salute to the Navy, for which she had us wearing sailor suits with jaunty red ties, white bell-bottoms, and hats. She didn't have to worry about Peggy and me running off with some beach bum. We didn't get a second look from even the bums. I take that back. They did give us a second look, but then they laughed and went back to looking at the noncloned girls on the beach.

I think I was about sixteen when I reached the mother-daughter saturation point. Mom had sprung her latest creations on us: three lavender, puffy-sleeved taffeta gowns and dyed-to-match satin pumps for us to wear to my cousin's wedding.

"Mom," I said as I stood on a stool while she pinned the hem of my gown, "I've decided to wear my pink knit dress to the wedding."

From the pained look on her face, I couldn't tell if she'd swallowed a pin or if I'd broken her heart. "But I don't have time to make Peggy and me dresses to match," she said.

"Peggy wants to wear her peach dress, and we think you should wear your cream suit. It's time, Mom."

Indeed, it was time. PDS does terrible things to a woman, and it had turned my mother into a sobbing lavender puddle in the middle of the dining room floor. It was then that I vowed never, ever to subject any future daughter to the effects of PDS. *There must be a vaccine,* I hoped.

Alas, there is none, as I discovered when I had daughters of my own. The Syndrome ran rampant through every church, every Mother's Day Out group, every PTA meeting. Everywhere women gathered, I'd hear them trading outfit-matching ideas. Only through sheer will power and much prayer did I manage to stay PDS-free for nearly eighteen years.

Recently I succumbed.

Although I take full responsibility for the consequences of my moral weakness, I do place some of the blame on the Nickerson family at church. They proved to be my undoing: five girls ranging in age from six months to twelve years (plus mom, Becky).

Every Sunday morning at 8:15, Becky led her brood—always dressed alike, always adorable—into the sanctuary. (Remember, that adorability factor will get you every time.)

"Aren't they cute?" I'd say to my daughters as we watched them file in.

Alison and Laura would nod, but by the look in their eyes, I could tell they were praying madly that I wouldn't contract that dreaded disease. They knew my childhood stories by heart. Too late. Despite my vows and all my prayers, PDS struck a few weeks before Mother's Day. It had been a while since I'd had my sewing machine out, and what with my Quest for Virtue and all, I'd been thinking about doing some sewing to fulfill verse 24: "She makes linen garments and sells them."

One night I went to bed thinking about the types of garments I should make, and the next morning I woke up humming the tune to the *Patty Duke Show* and thinking of the Nickerson girls in their blue seersucker jumpers.

"Wouldn't it be cute…," I said to myself. (For those unfamiliar with PDS, early warning signs include "wouldn't it be cute" musings and blatant disregard for the opinions of all others involved in your musings.)

Probably due to my age and exhaustion from all the years of fending off PDS, my immunity broke down, and I advanced rapidly to the "hop in the car and rush off to the fabric store" phase.

The disease hit me head-on as I leafed through the pattern books.

Finding something we all could wear was no small feat. I chose a form-fitting dress in a cream-and-cranberry floral with a scalloped neck, dropped waist, long puffy sleeves, and fanny-bows. Although it was a style and color none of us would have ever purposely chosen, it looked adorable on the mother-daughter models in the pattern book.

"And it'll look adorable on us," I mumbled through my PDS stupor as I drove home to my sewing machine.

Of one thing I was certain: My project had to be hush-hush. I wanted to surprise the girls on Mother's Day morning. I clung to the faint hope that when they saw the finished dresses, their hearts would melt in anticipation of yet another mother-daughter bonding opportunity.

Nearly every day for a week, as soon as the girls left for school, out came all my sewing paraphernalia. With my trusty Singer machine buzzing and whirring and the steam iron hissing, I'd stitch and press until just before they were due home, then I'd hide any evidence of cranberry dresses.

On the days I didn't sew, I combed the mall for the perfect accessories: cream satin ballet slippers and hose, antique golden lockets. I knew that after only one look at the three of us in those dresses, the girls would be hooked for life. No more dressing like individuals. (How passé.)

Mother's Day Eve arrived, and in a state of near-painful anticipation, I waited until both girls were asleep and set out our outfits for church the next morning.

"Surprise! Happy Mother's Day!" I yelled that next morning as I raced through the house waking everyone up. "What do you think?"

I'll spare you the details of the scene that followed. Let's just say the girls weren't exactly thrilled about being seen as a cranberry-floral, satin-slippered trio—especially with fanny bows. However, since the rule at our house is humor Mom on Mother's Day, my daughters, albeit reluctantly, put on their "geek dresses," as Alison called them, and trudged out to the car.

Despite my full-blown PDS state of euphoria, I sensed something was amiss. "Hair bows!" I cried and ran back into the house to get them. Once inside the house, I felt again that nagging sense of something not being right. I looked in the mirror and attached my hair bow to my short brown hair. A sense of foreboding clutched at my heart.

"You look like a geek," said a voice inside my head. "Your daughters look like geeks."

I covered my ears. "Make the voices go away!" I yelled, but the message continued. Finally I beckoned the girls back in the house and told them to change into their own clothes. Then, and only then, did the voices stop.

After that, all traces of my PDS disappeared. I was miraculously cured, divinely healed, and clearheaded enough once again to return my attention to my Quest. Meanwhile, the girls stuffed their dresses way back in the section of their closets they call "Never-*Never* Land."

Later that evening, as I pondered the "making and selling garments" verse, I began to weep. No, it wasn't a recurring attack of PDS. It wasn't even PMS. I wept because a few days earlier my neighbor Lydia had expressed an interest in becoming a VW—but Lydia couldn't sew.

"Oh, Lord," I cried into my hands. "What about Lydia? Will that exclude her from Virtue? Is there hope for my friend?"

I opened my Bible, hoping for an alternative clause for that particular verse. Technically, I didn't find one spelled out in black and white, but as I thought about the VW's life, I considered her industriousness. She did what she could with the skills she had, which happened to be sewing.

I sew, but Lydia can't. However, she—or any woman—can do other things. I know of women who make and sell crafts, clean other people's houses while their own children are in school, provide day care in their homes, type papers, work as freelance writers, editors, and artists. The possibilities are endless.

The Lord created us to work, whether it's in the home or outside, whether we get paid or not, and he will provide satisfying labor for our hands if we ask him.

"Even Lydia," I said, just in time too. Wouldn't you know it? The minute I said her name, she was at my door announcing a garage sale she was planning.

"Oh, Lydia!" I gave her a huge hug. "That's so industrious of you!" She smiled, then asked if I had anything I wanted to sell. I immediately remembered I hadn't completed the "and sells them" part of verse 24, so along with all the outdated and outgrown clothes in our closets, I handed over to Lydia the cranberry floral Mother's Day dresses.

On the day of the sale, I wandered over to Lydia's to help her out. While she and I stood around arranging sale items on tables, tragedy struck. Oh, not to me or Lydia; it happened to a customer. As a woman and her two daughters walked up the driveway, the mom took one look at the three dresses, and before she could utter, "Wouldn't it be cute…," she'd handed over three ten-dollar bills (twice my asking price) and walked off, not even bothering to try them on. Poor thing, she never even knew what hit her.

As they drove away, I overheard one of the daughters whining, "But, Mom, we'll look like…"

PDS strikes again.

Discovering Your Gift

After twelve years and 186,000 miles on my red Ford Tempo, I've decided I have the gift of driving girls. With two daughters and their assorted friends, it seems a natural fit. They need to get places, and I don't want them getting into strange cars driven by even stranger-looking boys nicknamed "Monster." Case closed.

If I were to identify my spiritual gift from the usual list, I'd have to say it falls into the category of "helps." I don't think twice about doing things like driving; I just do it because it needs doing and I enjoy it.

That's the beauty of a gift. It's a pleasure. It's God's pleasure to give each of his children one or more spiritual gifts to use for his glory within the body of believers and also in engaging with those outside the church. It's our pleasure to use them.

Perhaps you haven't yet discovered your particular gift. Here's a plan for launching your search:

1. List things you like to do or that come easily to you. (Hint: You don't need to think big. Something as simple as "I like to wash dishes after church functions" counts.)
2. Identify what you don't like to do or what you find difficult to do. Ask God to help you identify these things, and be honest.
3. Find ways to use your gift. This doesn't have to involve some grand plan; most gifts are used on a daily basis in all kinds of seemingly small ways that mean a great deal to the people on the receiving end.
4. Go forth and labor in joy.

Digging Deeper

1. Suppose a family in your neighborhood has fallen on hard times and someone else has suggested that the whole neighborhood help. What particular task would you choose? Which of the following would you most naturally enjoy doing: give money, clean their house, share the gospel, organize the help party, pray, sit and

listen quietly as the people talk? In what other ways would you consider helping?

2. In the following list of spiritual gifts taken from Romans 12 and 1 Corinthians 12, find the gifts that correspond to or complement your answers to the above questions.

    *   administration (management, organization)
    *   discernment (distinguishing truth from error)
    *   encouragement (comforting, inspiring, motivating)
    *   evangelism (sharing the gospel effectively)
    *   faith (an unwavering belief in the ability of God to work in any situation and the ability to inspire others)
    *   giving (generous with money and goods)
    *   helps (serving others, often behind the scenes)
    *   hospitality (setting people at ease; opening home freely)
    *   leadership (visionary, motivator)
    *   mercy (identifying with the suffering and offering help to ease pain)
    *   teaching (clearly presenting God's truth and inspiring others)

3. Are any of the gifts listed above more important than the others? (See Ephesians 4:4-5,16 and 1 Corinthians 12:12-27.) List the ways each of the gifts listed above can be used in a church and/or community.

4. Can you identify any other gifts that may be evident in your life? How can you use your gifts this week in your family? in your church? in your community?

~

"Stop trying to be what God didn't make you to be. Identifying what I'm not gifted in isn't 'low self-esteem.' It's simply the truth—and a

most freeing one. *Attending a million art classes will never make me an artist. There's no point in wasting energy there. My previous frustrations came from trying to do things God hadn't asked, nor equipped, me to do."*

—RUTH E. VAN REKEN, "If You Think You're Nothing Special, Think Again,"
Today's Christian Woman

Chapter 17

I Am Fearful, Hear Me Cluck

She can laugh at the days to come.

PROVERBS 31:25

I'm afraid I have a confession to make. Actually, that *is* my confession: I'm afraid. As in yellow-bellied, terror-stricken, *bwahk-bwahk* chicken. I'm scared of mountain roads, bridges, driving on holidays, and large groups of eighth-graders at the mall.

I'm afraid that if I get up to speak before an audience, no one will listen. Or if I try to say something profound, they'll laugh. Even worse, what if I try to say something funny and they don't laugh?

I'm afraid I might run into an alligator if I go for a walk around the lake. I'm afraid that if I do, I won't remember whether you're supposed to run away or lie down and play dead. I'm afraid my headaches are brain tumors, my sore throats are cancer, and my gas pains are appendicitis attacks.

I have a profound dread of eating broccoli or spinach in public. It's not so much the eating as the after-eating. I'm terrified of having green flecks caught between my teeth. I don't want to be at the table with someone, revealing the serious, intimate details of my life, only to have their attention focused on the broccoli in my teeth. To combat this phobia of mine, whenever broccoli is on the menu, I find a designated tooth-checker to whom I can grin and ask, "Do you see any green stuff?"

I'm deathly afraid of flying. Actually, I'm not afraid of flying—I'm afraid of crashing. Every time I get into an airplane, I take my white knuckles and flip through my Bible trying to find a "thy plane shall not end up in a field in Kansas" verse. As soon as we get up in the air, Barry always comforts me by saying, "Don't worry. One way or another, this plane's going to come down."

I have other fears too. I remember one time we arrived at JFK in New York City. (I forgot to mention my fear of New York.) As I waited for our luggage, Barry went to see about a rental car. Scared witless, I stood by a counter, trying to look invisible to all the muggers and bad guys who were out to get me.

Then I saw him.

A bearded man in a long overcoat and a furry hat (obviously a Russian spy) glanced around, looking strangely suspicious. My heart, beating out of my chest, rose into my throat as I watched him glance in my direction and nod, which I took as a signal for his goons to move in.

As the man walked over to the bank of pay phones near me, he slowly and deliberately opened his overcoat, undoubtedly to pull out an Uzi and shoot me. Although I didn't really want to make a scene, I didn't want my brains splattered all over the airport either. So, at the exact moment the man reached into his inside pocket, I screamed across the terminal, "Barry! Duck!" and hit the ground myself—as the man took out a piece of paper and proceeded to make a phone call.

All right, so I was wrong about the man in the furry hat. Just as I was wrong about the two guys in the convertible who, as they pulled up alongside our rental car, reached down for semiautomatic rifles—and brought up Popsicles from a cooler. I screamed, "Barry! Duck!" that time too.

I'm afraid my list of fears and phobias is exhaustive. And with the thought of them weighing heavily on my mind, I found myself at a loss as to what to do. How can I expect to attain Virtue if I'm so afraid of everything—including the future?

With fear and trembling I picked up my Bible and went out for a walk.

"Lions and tigers and bears, oh my," I recited as I walked down the trail by the lake.

"Which one are you?" asked a raspy voice from behind me.

I stood frozen in my tracks, waiting for something terrible to happen. When nothing did, I turned around to find Earl, a spry, elderly gentleman who lives near me, sitting on the ground and tapping the dirt off his Converse hi-tops with his cane.

"Earl, you scared me! What are you doing down there?"

"Just resting. Well, which one are you? A lion, a tiger, or a bear?" He brushed off his gray sweat suit and adjusted his New York Yankees baseball cap, then patted the ground next to him. "Have a seat."

After inspecting the dirt for red ants, brown recluse spiders, and any other creepy crawlies that might slither inside my jeans and bite me with poisonous venom, I swept aside some dried leaves and sat down.

"I'm none of the above," I told him. "I'm a chicken."

After explaining to him about my nearly yearlong quest for Virtue, I opened my Bible and showed him my latest verse: "She can laugh at the days to come."

"According to this," I said, "to be Truly Virtuous, I have to be fearless. And I'm afraid I'll never pass this one because…well, because *I'm afraid.*"

"Well, missy," Earl said, "what I usually do when I'm afraid of somethin' is to write it all down on paper. That way, I can look my fear right square in the eye. Somehow, just seein' puny letters on a piece o' paper puts my fears into perspective. Ain't nothin' on no piece o' paper can compare with almighty God."

"I guess you're right, Earl," I said as I rose to my feet and dusted myself off. "I'll let you know if I ever reach the Ultimate V."

With that, we parted, Earl continuing down the trail and me skipping off back home. Once I was back at my desk, I sat down and made a list of all my fears. Here are just a few:

They'll Find Me Nakedaphobia. It's the fear of the "Oh, gross!"

response from paramedics. We used to live in California where earthquakes are common. Whenever I'd get into the shower, my immediate thought would be, "Please, God, don't let there be an earthquake right now." While the possibility of the ceiling crashing on my head scared me, I was more afraid of being found naked, prompting some guy to say to his partner, "Oh gross! Hey, Chuck, come look at this."

Similarly, Leg Hairaphobia is the fear of being in an accident when you haven't shaved your legs for five days.

Fashion Don'taphobia. I am terrified that if I open a women's magazine, I'll find my picture (eyes blocked off of course) on their Fashion Dos and Don'ts page—as a Don't. I know it'll show me wearing my dingy Otter Pops T-shirt; my frayed, faded jeans; half-melted-off makeup; and my "groovy shoes" (holey, dirty slip-ons). It's a sad commentary on my life, but this is my favorite outfit to wear on days I don't plan to go anywhere. The only trouble is, I usually end up going somewhere, like to the market or the library. Just the other day I overheard one of my daughter's friends tell her, "Alison, I didn't know your mom's into the grunge look."

T.P.aphobia. I know this is stupid, but I'm afraid to go into the store and buy just toilet paper. I know everybody goes to the bathroom and everybody uses toilet paper; I just don't want anyone to know that *I* do. I don't think I'm alone on this one either. I have this theory that whenever someone brings five items up to the cashier, and one of those items is a package of toilet paper, he or she probably only needed the T.P. and was afraid to buy just *that*. Which is why I always make it a point to buy at least twelve things, twenty to be safe. (Hey, it's my phobia, and I'll tremble if I want to.)

As I finished my list, I realized some phobias are actually beneficial. For instance, Dirty Windowaphobia would cause its sufferers to keep their windows clean. Run Out of Gasaphobics would keep their tanks filled. See what I mean?

But then there are the stomach-knotting, anxiety-producing, shaking-in-your-Reeboks fears that only serve to paralyze phobics such as myself.

For instance, being afraid to try new things because I may fail—or being afraid I may succeed. I'm afraid of the phone ringing late at night, that it might bring bad news. I'm afraid to let my children go off into a world wrought with muggings, carjackings, and blatant disregard for human life.

I'm afraid that if I let people know who I really am they will be repulsed. I'm afraid of being left alone, of being misunderstood, and of not being perfect.

"Okay, Earl, here goes," I said, then took a long look at my list. As I read over each fear, I remembered that Franklin Roosevelt once said, "The only thing we have to fear is fear itself." *I'm afraid he's right,* I thought. In my nearly forty phobic years, I'd learned that during those times when I've been in genuine danger, I've rarely been afraid. God has always given me his peace.

Of course, knowing that poses a whole new set of fears and phobias. I've found that whenever I experience complete peace, I start worrying that God has given me peace because something bad is about to happen! (Do you think there's such a thing as No Fearaphobia?)

I looked again at my list. If I wanted to be like Madam Thirty-One, I couldn't let my fears hinder me. I thought about a friend who always says to go toward your fear and face it head-on. I toyed with that thought for a while.

"I'll do it!" I shouted. "The very next Florida snowstorm I'm going to hop on the nearest plane, and I think I'll rassle a boa the next time I see one at the city pool."

However, in order to fulfill my "laughing at the days to come" verse, I had to do something then and there. And I did. That very day I faced one of my biggest fears head-on.

We ran out of toilet paper.

Fear? NOT!

When it comes to being fearful, I'm afraid I'm not alone. I have a friend who's so afraid of elevators that she trudged up three flights of hospital stairs—while in labor. To someone who isn't afraid of elevators, such behavior sounds absurd, but to someone trapped by fear, it makes perfect, logical sense.

"Fear makes us prisoners within ourselves," writes H. Norman Wright in *Quiet Times for Couples.* "It makes life a chore. It disables and cripples our relationships with others. Fear saps our energy and interferes with our progress in life."

Fear keeps us from living the abundant life that Jesus promised his followers. However, the secret to overcoming fear is not avoiding it, but facing it head-on.

I keep this quote from Ralph Waldo Emerson near my desk: "Do the thing you fear and the death of fear is certain." Mental health specialists call it exposure therapy. God calls it faith. We pray and ask him to take our fear away. Instead, he tells us to get on that elevator or airplane and trust that his "perfect love casts out fear" (1 John 4:18, NASB).

He does that because he knows that when we choose faith over fear, our fear shrinks before us. It may never go away completely, but it will lose its power to paralyze.

Digging Deeper

1. Name some of your fears. Which are legitimate and which are irrational? What are the probabilities of what you fear actually happening?
2. According to 1 John 4:18, what is the root of fear? Look up the following verses: Psalms 27:1-6; 34:4-10; Isaiah 43:1-5; Luke 12:4-7; Romans 8:15-16,31-33. What comfort can you find in these verses for your fearful heart?
3. Have you ever faced one of your fears head-on? What happened? List some of the fears you want to conquer. Ask God to help you and trust that he will. Remember, you have not been given a

spirit of fear, "but of power and of love and of a sound mind" (2 Timothy 1:7, NKJV).

4. The *Bible for Today's Christian Woman* admonishes, "See God as your Savior, not as a saboteur." Read Psalm 91 slowly. Personalize it as your prayer to God today.

~

"We are inwardly constructed in nerve and tissue, brain cell and soul, for faith and not for fear. God made us that way. To live by worry is to live against reality."

—DR. E. STANLEY JONES

Chapter 18

I Can't Believe I Said That!

She speaks with wisdom.

PROVERBS 31:26

Seven-twenty-eight A.M. As I sat at my dining room table with my Bible open to page 696, panic gripped me. Of all the virtuous attributes of Lady Proverbs, speaking with wisdom was undoubtedly the one with which I was least familiar. To tell you the truth, I'd never done it before. It's not that I hadn't done a lot of speaking. My mom claims I was born talking and haven't stopped since. I talk loud. I talk fast. I talk when no one's listening. I speak about things I'm an expert on. I speak about things I know nothing about.

Mostly though, I speak with my foot in my mouth. You see, I suffer from I-Can't-Believe-I-Said-That Syndrome. Symptoms include constant gasping (by the woman afflicted with the syndrome after something stupid flies out of her mouth and also by the one afflicted by the stupid something), hand-to-mouth reflex (in a futile attempt to cap the stupidity, postemission), and head shaking as the ICBIST sufferer says, "I can't believe I said that!" (A variation on that theme is the listener shaking her head and saying, "I can't believe YOU said that!")

As an ICBISTer, I say things like, "Poodles aren't real dogs" (to someone who, unbeknownst to me, is a proud poodle owner). Or I'll be in a shoe store and pick up a size-ten shoe and say, "Look at these boats." Nine times out of ten, the person I say this to (or an innocent bystander) wears that size.

Same thing goes for "I'd never be caught dead (buying, wearing, doing, reading, eating) that." If I say I'd never be caught dead buying crocheted toilet-paper covers at the church fall bazaar, I'm sure to be talking to the woman who crochets them.

If I say I'd never be caught dead reading a romance novel, you can pretty much bet that I'm talking to a romance novel writer. You might think talking with your foot in your mouth is an impossibility, but let me assure you, it's not. I do it all the time. Just a few weeks ago I met a man at the gym who told me he'd been a bodybuilder for forty-eight years. Since he didn't look Arnold Schwarzeneggerish, I asked him, "When did you stop?"

Although he laughed, I could tell by the look on his face I'd committed a major faux pas. It wasn't until I was halfway home that I realized my question was the equivalent of his asking me, "So when did you let yourself go?"

My most common blunders usually involve pregnant friends, or even strangers. "You two must not get out much," I've said to a woman expecting her fourth baby in five years. Or I'll say, "Wow! You're soooo big!" forgetting what it was like to be pregnant and feeling like a bloated semitruck. The last thing I wanted was to be reminded that I looked like a beachball with legs.

Worse than commenting on a pregnant friend's big belly is asking, "When's the baby due?" to someone who's not pregnant. I've yet to find a graceful way to get out of that one. It's too bad life isn't like camcorders, which allow you to push a rewind button and record over your mistakes.

Although I haven't discovered an antidote, having a taste of my own medicine has proved to be an effective vaccine. Once I attended a conference wearing a big dress. Halfway through the day I didn't feel well and asked a gentleman where I could lie down. He took one look at my dress, led me to a back pew in the sanctuary, then called in a nurse because he was sure I was about to deliver a baby right then and there. A buzz went around the conference, "Some lady's in the sanctuary giving birth."

After I assured the seven or so people who came to help me that my distress was only caused by too much coffee, I still had to face several dozen well-meaning strangers who questioned me about my false alarm. "Thank you for asking," I said, "but I'm not pregnant. I'm just wearing a big dress."

I'll tell you one thing, if I gained nothing else from that conference, I learned never to assume anything about anybody (or at least not voice my assumptions). I also learned never to wear that dress again.

I thought I'd have the opportunity to redeem myself, and maybe even fulfill my "speaking with wisdom" requirement, the day my Bible study leader asked me to fill in for her.

"It's easy," she said. "Just read the passage and open it up for discussion."

Well, that's too easy, I thought. *I'll prepare a brilliant lesson and dazzle everyone with my wisdom. Wait till they hear what I have to say!*

Our key verse was 1 Corinthians 9:27: "But [like a boxer] I buffet my body" (AMP). I chose to expound on this little-discussed concept of "buffeting" the body, using poster-size photos of the salad bar at Sizzler's as visual aids. As I stood before my audience (actually only five other women from my church), I began by comparing life to a buffet where we have our choice of everything underneath the sneeze guard.

"But if we eat too much of the wrong things," I said, "our life will be out of balance." About the time I started comparing onions to the bitter things of life and croutons to little toasty bits of the Word of God, a twitter went around the room.

One woman, Darcy, raised her hand. "Isn't that word 'buffet,' as in hitting or beating?"

I felt my body turn crimson, from my toes on up to my head. I looked around for a place to hide, while at the same time trying to save (my red) face.

"Why yes, Darcy," I said, stuffing my visual aids underneath my chair and covering my face with my open Bible, "I suppose that's one way of interpreting it."

Everyone laughed; I eventually laughed, but inwardly I cringed. Later, on the way home from lunch (ironically, the salad bar at Sizzler's), I drove alone in mortified, wisdomless silence, vowing never to speak again. Ever. Never, ever.

I would've succeeded too, if it hadn't been for the following Sunday morning when the toilet overflowed for the sixty jillionth time. One of our oak trees' roots regularly clogged up our plumbing lines, causing tsunami-like waves of toilet water to flood the house. (Note: We've since had the problem corrected.)

We woke up that morning to the all-too-familiar stench and ankle-deep standing water. The routine when that happened was to bail out the water, mop up the floors, and throw out whatever got ruined. However, that morning I flat-out didn't want to. I was tired of it and secretly blamed everything on my husband (who was out of town at the time). Things like that always happen when he's gone. Instead of dealing with the mess, all I wanted to do was get out of there and escape to church, where I wouldn't have to cope with anything for a few hours.

As the girls and I were getting into the car, my neighbor, out getting her morning newspaper, came over to say hello. She noticed the open windows and the pile of soggy bath towels on the porch. "Another flood?" she asked.

I threw my head back and laughed. "Yeah—surf's up!" I told her. "But you know what, Mrs. Baker? It doesn't matter because I'm going to church."

Here's where the speaking with wisdom happened. Actually, that was it, and I didn't even realize what I'd said until a couple of weeks later. Long after I'd cleaned up everything and had forgotten I'd said anything at all, Mrs. Baker came over to tell me that because of my "cheerful acceptance" of my circumstances and such total devotion to God that all I could think about was going to church, *she* couldn't stop thinking about it. She glowed as she told me, "Guess what? We're all going to church together this Sunday, thanks to what you said!"

Ultimately, as unbelievable as it sounds, she and two of her adult children recommitted their lives to Christ, and her husband recently expressed an interest in joining them in their faith. Every time I see her, she mentions my "words of wisdom."

Huh?

I find it odd that the words containing the greatest wisdom are often the ones I'm not even aware of speaking. Maybe God plans it that way so I don't get all puffed up with pride (as I'm apt to do) and talk about biblical buffets.

I know there's hope for me yet. After all, the Bible talks about how God once used a talking donkey to speak with wisdom to a stubborn Balaam. If he can use one donkey, then surely he can use me.

Fool's Wisdom

Someone once said, "Experience comes from what we have done, but wisdom comes from what we have done badly." If that's true, then I am the wisest woman on earth.

The Proverbs Thirty-One Woman spoke with wisdom. Maybe that came from putting her foot in her mouth one too many times or learning that washing a feather pillow works much better if you sew up the tears in the seams first. However, that kind of wisdom anybody with half a brain could achieve. I think the kind of wisdom the passage talks about is the wisdom that comes only from God.

"There is a way that seems right to a man," writes King Solomon, "but in the end it leads to death" (Proverbs 14:12). This reminds me of some so-called wisdom I once gave to a friend. I was only nineteen at the time and didn't know the wisdom of God, but that's no excuse. I counseled a friend to pursue a relationship with a married man, saying, "When love comes, you can't worry about obstacles."

Worldly wisdom says, "If it feels good, do it." Date or marry that unbeliever; leave that husband who doesn't make you happy anymore. However, the end of such wisdom is death—sometimes for your body, always for your soul.

Godly wisdom, as defined by Larry Crabb, is "the belief that accepting God's way, no matter how painful, leads to ultimate joy." Foolishness is refusing to believe that "going our way, even though it genuinely relieves distress and feels good, leads ultimately to despair."

God's wisdom often sounds foolish and hokey in today's world, but it's the only wisdom that gives life.

Digging Deeper

1. What are some "words of wisdom" commonly spoken in today's society that contradict God's wisdom?

2. Read the following Scripture passages: Proverbs 2; 3:13-22; 8:12-21,32-35; 9:10-12; 1 Corinthians 1:30; Colossians 2:2-3. What do these verses teach you about wisdom?

3. Read James 3:13-18. How can you tell the difference between earthly wisdom and the wisdom that comes from heaven?

4. Is there a situation in your life for which you need wisdom? Read the following passages to learn how you can gain the wisdom you desire: Psalm 1:1-3; Proverbs 3:5-6; 22:17; James 1:5-6.

―❦―

"Our desire to be wise must spring from a heart whose sole purpose is to know our awesome God and to please him, not self. For I believe that as we truly seek his wisdom from above, then all the characteristics of wisdom will begin to be manifested in our lives."

—CYNTHIA HEALD, *Becoming a Woman of Excellence*

Chapter 19

The Sum Total of My Knowledge

Faithful instruction is on her tongue.

PROVERBS 31:26

Some days you just wake up in a fog. You can't remember your name or what day it is. You hit your toe on the dresser, and as you hop down the hall in pain, you step on the cat, and she claws your leg. The granola spills between the stove and the refrigerator, there's no milk for your coffee, somebody put the ice cream carton in the pantry cupboard so ants have convened from as far away as Macon, Georgia—and it's all downhill from there.

But not that day. That day I woke up well rested and sang Broadway show tunes while I showered and dressed. The cat hadn't thrown up anywhere, raccoons hadn't tipped over our trash cans, and the pimple on my chin had disappeared. Not only that, my hair did just what I wanted it to do. Yep, it was an all-around good hair day.

"Oh, what a beautiful morning," I sang as I poured myself a cup of coffee and prepared to face my verse for the day: "Faithful instruction is on her tongue." I'd peeked at the verse before I went to bed and spent the night dreaming about it. As a result, I woke up oozing with faithful instruction, and my tongue was itching to pass it on.

I called Kathy.

"Sweetie, how are you?" she cried. "*Qué pasa* and all that?"

"Kathy, you wouldn't believe how many verses I've checked off my list. I can speak with wisdom—well, I did it once—and I kept my lamp burning late at night, and I sold some dresses, and I even bought myself a new outfit. I feel like I can do anything the VW did!"

"Oh, sweetie, I'm sooo happy to hear that. Are you really able to laugh at the future, unafraid? No fears left? Did you go on an airplane yet?"

"Well, not exactly—"

"Oh, by the way," she interrupted, "I saw your husband the other day out by the city gate. You know how I hate to criticize, but his shirt looked a bit raggedy. I thought the VW's husband was supposed to be some sort of bastion of taste and style."

"Well, hers might've been, but Barry likes to be comfortable."

"I suppose… So anyway, sweetie, tell me what's going on now."

I blurted out, "That's why I called you! I've got some faithful instruction on my tongue that I want to pass on." I took a breath and continued. "Kathy, picture this: I'm sixteen years old and bored, so I flip on the television. Nothing's on except a craft demonstration, so I sit down to watch some lady make candles by pouring melted wax in sand. It looks like fun, so I call to my mother (who's upstairs taking a nap) that I'm going to the store and will be right back.

"When I return home with my blocks of wax and red crayons, I set them on the stove to melt, then go out to the backyard to dig a hole in my sister's sandbox, unaware of the fact that when wax reaches a certain temperature, it flashes and catches on fire. I learn this when I return to the kitchen and find my wax is now flambéed."

"Is that your little faithful instruction?" she asked.

"Just let me finish. I run upstairs to my mother (who by now is in the shower) and wait until the water stops to tell her we have a small kitchen emergency—a *minor* mishap, possibly involving a flame or two. She screams something inaudible that I take to mean, 'You better get downstairs and put out the fire and clean up the mess before I get there, or *else.*'

"I race back downstairs and throw a box of baking soda on my burning wax. I now have powdered red wax everywhere: on the cupboards, on the countertops, on the stove, on the floor. I scrape and scrub with all my might, and by the time my mom comes downstairs, the kitchen is back to normal. All except for a huge pot of (ruined) melted red wax. Mom tells me she's going out for a few minutes and warns me not to get into any more trouble. I promise her I won't, but inadvertently I do. Not knowing what else to do with the wax, I dump it down the sink, then run the cold water.

"Then I panic.

"The wax hardens inside the pipes. The water from the dishwasher gushes out onto the kitchen floor; the washing machine out in the garage heaves and groans, then its water floods out the bottom; and then the downstairs toilet overflows. By the time Mom returns, I'm ankle-deep in water and praying she won't notice.

"She notices, calls the plumber, then calls my dad at work. Dad comes home, carrying a BIG wrench. Then the plumber arrives, also with a big wrench. After they do whatever it is plumbers and dads do to get red wax out of pipes, the plumber hands me a perfect pipe-shaped candle, and my dad hands me the plumber's bill. We all live happily ever after because from that moment on, I never make candles ever again."

I paused to let my story sink in. After several seconds of silence, Kathy said, "Sweetie, I don't get your point. Why are you telling me this story?"

"Because," I said, "just like the VW, I, too, have some faithful instruction on my tongue that I can pass on! Never pour hot wax down the sink. Or if you do, make sure you add a wick, so when the plumber hands you your $437 candle, you can at least light it and get your money's worth. What do you think?"

I couldn't see Kathy's face, but I could picture her tapping her chin as she always did before one of her grand pronouncements. "Why didn't you simply go down to the Dollar Store and buy a dozen red candles for seventy-nine cents? It would've saved you a ton of trouble."

"Kathy, you're missing the point—I've got faithful instruction on my tongue to pass on just like the VW. I'm that much closer to Virtuehood!"

"Well, sweetie, that's as cute as a button and all, and I thank you for sharing your little story with me, but I have to dash off now. Ta ta."

"Ta ta," I answered and hung up. "I don't care what anyone says," I shouted. "I can do this one!" After crossing verse 26 off my list, I went through my address book, calling each of my friends and passing on all of my faithful instruction. Here's what I told them:

- Unless you want it to come out your nose, don't laugh and drink soda at the same time.

- No matter how bad the flea problem, don't spray Raid on your dog. Sure, the fleas will come right up to the surface all nice and dead, but your dog will start making funny sounds like the time your cousin Steve got a piece of pretzel stuck in his right tonsil and kept making those disgusting hocking noises while you were all trying to watch *The Wizard of Oz,* and your Aunt Rita kept yelling at your Uncle Al, "See, I told you we shoulda had his tonsils out."

- Mayonnaise makes great hair conditioner. However, if you wrap your mayonnaisey head in plastic while you sleep, your body heat will turn the mayo rancid.

- Don't believe anyone who tells you that drinking a cup of vinegar a day will melt away your fat. All it does is make you feel like a pickle from the inside out and cause your breath to smell like a jar of gherkins.

- Remember where you park, especially at Disney World, where they name their parking places after Disney characters. Nothing's worse than walking around the Disney lot thinking you're "Happy" when, in fact, you're "Dopey."

- Don't let your car know when you have some extra money. Same thing goes for your furnace, water heater, and septic tank.
- No matter what the diet books say, when you're craving a Snickers candy bar, munching carrot sticks doesn't satisfy—unless you dip them in hot fudge and roll them in chopped, salted peanuts. Even then you have to wash them down with chocolate milk.
- If you have a choice between taking out the trash or letting it sit down in the basement and forgetting about it until it produces more maggots than you thought ever existed on earth—choose taking out the trash.
- Don't shop for bathing suits with anyone whose hips are smaller than yours.
- Unless you like a dull finish, don't wash your car with bleach. Neither should you use bleach for washing out your fishbowl, unless you like your pet fish floating belly-side up. Do, however, use bleach to remove mildew from the shower, but don't forget to wipe your feet off before you run on your dark gray carpeting to answer the phone (unless you like the look of white footprints down the hall).

Other faithful instruction is on my tongue as well. For instance, chewing on a cheap pen during church causes blue teeth and lips (and the people around you to twitter); instructions should be read before putting the semipermanent dye goop on your just-permed locks; and when you're turning screws or knobs, it's "righty tighty, lefty loosey."

However faithful that instruction may be, the most faithful instruction I have to pass on is the Word of God. Among other things, it tells me to cast all my cares upon the Lord (1 Peter 5:7) and instructs me to stand firm in the faith (1 Peter 5:9). It also tells me not to stand in the path of sinners (Psalm 1:1) but to stand in awe of God (Ecclesiastes 5:7).

The Bible encourages me to draw near to God with a sincere heart (Hebrews 10:22) and to be content (Philippians 4:11), diligent (1 Timothy

4:15), and strong in the grace that is in Christ Jesus (2 Timothy 2:1). Over all these virtues, I'm to put on love, which binds them all together in perfect unity (Colossians 3:14).

Oh…one final piece of instruction:

Throw out poppy seeds that move.

A Woman of the Book

In order for faithful instruction to be on my tongue, it first has to go into my mind and heart. As Jesus said, the things that come out of the mouth come from the heart (Matthew 15:18). However, I dare not trust my heart apart from the Word of God. Even as a redeemed child of God, my heart still has the capacity for great evil. Left to my own devices, the instruction I give to others may be tainted with my self-centered perceptions or tinged by my ignorance. No matter what I believe "truth" to be, if it's not based on the Word of God, it's not *the* truth—and there can only be one truth. Therefore, the only pure instruction I can confidently pass on to others is the very Word of God.

The Reverend Finis Jennings Dake wrote of the Bible,

> It is a book that contains the mind of God, the state of
> man, the way of salvation, the doom of sinners, and the
> happiness of believers. Its doctrines are holy, its precepts
> binding, its histories true, and its decisions immutable.
> Read it to be wise, believe it to be safe, and practice it to
> be holy. It contains light to direct you, food to support you,
> and comfort to cheer you. It is the traveler's map, the
> pilgrim's staff, the pilot's compass, the soldier's sword, and
> the Christian's charter.
>
> Here Heaven is opened, and the gates of Hell disclosed.
> Christ is its grand subject, our good its design, and the

glory of God its end. It should fill your memory, rule your heart, and guide your feet in righteousness and true holiness. Read it slowly, frequently, prayerfully.... It is a mine of wealth, the source of health, and a world of pleasure.

To be a woman of the Book, I must read it, meditate on it. I must let it dwell in me richly, transform my life, and be my food. I'm called to learn it and live it—and pass it on.

Digging Deeper

1. What reasons do people often give for not reading the Bible? Is spending time in God's Word a priority for you? Why or why not? When you do take time to read the Bible, what differences do you notice in your day? What Scripture passages have been particularly meaningful in your life? Why?

2. Why is studying God's Word important? Look up the following verses, and list what the Word of God accomplishes in a person's life: Deuteronomy 8:3; Psalms 19:7-11; 119:11,92-93; Proverbs 28:4; Ephesians 5:26; 1 Thessalonians 2:13; Hebrews 4:12; 1 Peter 1:23.

3. In the Garden of Eden, Eve was deceived by the serpent (Genesis 3:13). The apostle Paul writes about "weak-willed women, who are loaded down with sins and are swayed by all kinds of evil desires, always learning but never able to acknowledge the truth" (2 Timothy 3:6-7). Given our vulnerability to Satan's deception, we need to become intimately familiar with the characteristics of truth. Note what the following scriptures say about truth: Isaiah 45:19; John 1:14,17; 16:13; 17:17; Romans 1:22-25, 2:7-8; 2 Thessalonians 2:9-15; 1 John 2:3-5.

4. Martin Luther said he studied the Bible in the same way he gathered apples:

First, I shake the whole tree that the ripest may fall. Then I shake each limb, and when I have shaken each limb, I shake each branch and every twig. Then I look under every leaf; I search the Bible as a whole like shaking the whole tree. Then I shake every limb— study book after book. Then I shake every branch, giving attention to the chapters. Then I shake every twig, or a careful study of paragraphs and sentences and words and their meanings.

Choose a book of the Bible and get "shaking."

~

"The grass withers and the flowers fall, but the word of the Lord stands forever."

—1 PETER 1:24-25

Chapter 20

Am I My House's Keeper?

She watches over the affairs of her household.

Proverbs 31:27

Correct me if I'm wrong, but I'm guessing you wouldn't find a week-old plate of mashed potatoes on top of the VW's bookcase. I doubt she ever had a menagerie of antique roly-poly bugs behind her toilet or gunky refrigerator magnets. I'd even bet my life savings that you wouldn't find pink slimy stuff in her shower.

I'm ashamed to say you would find all those things at my house. Oh, I'm not a total slob. On the surface—albeit a dusty surface—my house appears to be clean. I subscribe to the "uh-oh, somebody's coming to the door, shove everything in the closets, and I'll deal with it later" school of housekeeping. It works well, until the closets get full and opening them becomes hazardous to your head (because of falling baseball cleats).

I have good intentions. Every spring I think about doing a thorough cleaning. I've even made lists of things I intend to do. The trouble is, here in Florida, spring lasts only about three and a half hours, usually on a Wednesday afternoon, and that's when I'm carpooling girls to softball practice.

So the crud underneath the refrigerator gets cruddier, and the glop between the stove and the counter gets gloppier. There just aren't enough hours in the day to do all that needs to be done.

It's not easy being a contemporary VW, especially with a busy family.

163

Take Barry, for example, who leaves his plastic coffee stirring thingies on top of the dresser, drops his work boots right by the front door, and rolls up and tosses his dirty socks at the nearest moving target (usually me). Or consider Laura, who (though I can't prove it) just picks up one end of her room and shakes it like an Etch-A-Sketch until every drawer falls open, every book flies off her shelf, and every paper she's ever come in contact with since kindergarten lies scattered on her bedroom floor.

And that's what it looks like AFTER she cleans it.

Add to that Alison's trail of empty soda cans and cereal bowls, grape stems and cherry pits, Band-Aid wrappers and algebra homework. Of course, I can't say I'm any better. My contributions are the piles of notes and file folders of papers that I keep in stacks from one end of the house to the other, all over the floor, or scattered across the dining room table.

Throw in the ironing board that stays set up in the middle of the living room, a never-depleted pile of laundry on the laundry room floor, empty toilet paper tubes sitting on the bathroom window sill because no one seems to know how to throw them away, and the ever-present toothpaste blob on the bathroom door.

Total all that up, toss in a cat that throws up regularly in the hallway, add a backpack here and a full wastebasket there, and you have what's generally termed a pigsty.

O Virtuous Woman, O Virtuous Woman. How didst thou do it—and all without a Dust Buster or Lemon Fresh Pledge?

One day last month I couldn't take it any longer. The affairs of my household had gone awry. Dust and disorder had run amok. Someone had spelled "Dust Me" in the grime on the coffee table, the ring around the bathtub had sprouted, a waxy yellow buildup had sprung up on my no-wax floors, and whenever I turned on the ceiling fans, our house took on the appearance of a windstorm on the dusty plains of Oklahoma.

I turned to my Bible and studied my proverb for that day: "She watches over the affairs of her household."

But how does one do it? How does one control those Clutter Monsters and detonate those Dirt Demons? As I mulled it over (and watched a pile of laundry multiply before my eyes), I remembered that when I was a girl, one woman on our block with a bunch of kids always kept her house ship-shape. The rumor was, she wanted to join the navy after her third or fourth baby, but the recruiter told her she was too old.

So she had about five more kids, called them her "squadron," and taught them how to spit-polish the "latrine" (bathroom). In spite of nine or ten kids, her house always sparkled.

Her secret hung around her neck. She had a whistle.

TWEEEEEEEET! went my whistle one bright Saturday morning at 0700 hours. "All right, you maggots!" I yelled through the hallway. "Move it, move it, move it! Swab them decks, mateys, and make that galley shine! I want to see nothing but elbows and backsides! Now, move it, move it, move it!"

Unfortunately, my troops weren't familiar with military maneuvers. Instead, they mutinied and went AWOL, taking my whistle with them and leaving me to face my monsters and demons alone.

This called for desperate action.

Still in my military mode, I donned a set of Barry's old air force fatigues and readied my plan of action. First strike: Remove Clutter's stronghold by ruthlessly throwing out everything that wasn't vital to human existence.

Four Hefty garbage bags later, mission accomplished—at least in the living room. Twelve Hefties later, I'd completely conquered Clutter.

Next strike: Nuke the dirt. I swept and scrubbed, buffed and polished. The footprint on the wall behind Laura's door? Gone. The dust clogging the bottom grate on the refrigerator? No more. Gone also were the grease splatters on the kitchen cupboards, Barry's whiskers in the bathroom sink, and the gunk around the kitchen faucet. No more cobwebs on Alison's ceiling, no more dead flies on top of the china hutch.

Good-bye, mold; so long, mildew. Adios, ring around the tub. By the time everyone returned, the house was exactly the way I'd always wanted it to be—and I was determined to keep it that way.

When everyone came in, they noticed the transformation and were duly impressed. AND, as I had hoped, they tried their hardest to maintain our home's newly pristine condition. They tiptoed around, putting things away and cleaning up after themselves.

But…things were not normal. It was almost as if they were afraid to touch anything. The whole thing reminded me of visiting my Great Aunt Sophia, who smelled of bleach and kept plastic covers on all her furniture. We weren't allowed to touch anything and could only sit on folding chairs on the back porch. To eat a cookie, we had to spread newspapers on the floor underneath our chairs, and we couldn't use the guest towels in any of the bathrooms.

When I started following my family around with a dustpan and whisk broom and dabbing bleach behind my ears, I knew I'd gone too far. Our house wasn't a home anymore. The next day I ordered Barry to drop his work boots by the front door and the girls to leave their backpacks in the dining room.

"Aah," I sighed.

"Aah," sighed two happy daughters and a happy husband.

"Now this doesn't mean we can all live slobbily ever after," I said. "It just means we have to find a balance somewhere."

The Virtuous Woman knew such balance. Proverbs 31 doesn't say she whirled around like a Tasmanian devil in a cleaning frenzy, doing everything herself and ending up defeated and exhausted. Neither does it say she was overwhelmed by her tasks and refused to do anything at all (ending up in the same defeated state). Rather, she managed the affairs of her family, overseeing every aspect of her home and the people in it. She knew how to delegate responsibility.

To be honest, I have a hard time finding a balance. My biggest problem is taking on everything myself mainly because it's easier than taking the time to show the girls how to do it or contending with their excuses and laments. ("But, Mom, I have homework!" "But, Mom, I'm tired!" "But, Mom, this is my favorite TV show!")

I tend to make excuses for them myself ("Well, Alison worked late last night," or "Laura's young"), but I've finally realized that I'm actually doing them a disservice by not requiring them to work around the house. Part of my job as "household affairs manager" is to see that my girls know how to fold a fitted bottom sheet and clean out a dryer lint trap so that when they leave home they'll be equipped to manage the affairs of their own households.

Actually, managing a home is much more than vacuuming Rice Krispies off the rug or scouring the ring from the tub. It's arranging dental appointments, signing field-trip permission slips, and monitoring the supply of brown paper lunch bags. It's French braiding hair, dropping off (and picking up!) dry cleaning, getting everyone to Sunday school in one piece, and being curator of the refrigerator art display. It's everything we as moms do, just because we're moms and that's how God made us.

As for keeping my house spotless at all times, I'm afraid that's highly unlikely as long as a living, breathing family resides here. Besides, when you think about it, fingerprints on the walls and muddy footprints on the tile aren't so bad when they're made by the people you love.

So pass me a sponge.

Better yet, call Alison and Laura for me…

The Unbalanced…Fall

I tend toward the all-or-nothing school of doing anything. When I cook, I make enough to feed several elephants. When I clean, I spit-shine and polish even the bottles of cleanser products. Then I rope off my cleaned rooms and prohibit anyone from entering.

I have what I call "no body parts" zones. These are areas of the house no body parts are allowed to touch: certain towels in the bathroom, certain pillows on the bed, a chair in my bedroom. I go ballistic when I see evidence of someone violating this rule.

On the other end of the spectrum are the times when I go days—weeks!—without even acknowledging the layers of dust building up on my furniture—or on my family. Either extreme makes me stressed, and stress makes me unbalanced, and being unbalanced makes me fall.

The words of Jesus describe me when he asks: "Are you tired? Worn out? Burned out…? Come to me. Get away with me and you'll recover your life. I'll show you how to take a real rest. Walk with me and work with me—watch how I do it. Learn the unforced rhythms of grace. I won't lay anything heavy or ill-fitting on you. Keep company with me and you'll learn to live freely and lightly" (Matthew 11:28-30, MSG).

A balanced life begins with acknowledging our stress, our "unbalance," and then seeking a steady foothold at the feet of Jesus. In the story of the two sisters, Mary and Martha of Bethany, Jesus commended Mary for choosing "what is better" as she sat at his feet while Martha frantically rattled pots and pans in the kitchen (Luke 10:42).

It's not that he loved Martha any less. He was simply pointing out that what she needed—what we need to find the peace and strength necessary to go about the life to which we are called—is to choose the "better" way, the restful way. When we do, we are kept from falling.

That's the best way to live.

Digging Deeper

1. When it comes to managing a home (excluding her financial dealings), Martha Stewart seems to me the epitome of perfection. (She makes her own marshmallows!) On a "Martha Stewart scale of perfect domesticity," with Martha being a perfect 10, where would you rate your home management skills? Which areas of home management are your strengths? Which are your weak areas?

2. Read Luke 10:38-42, then in your own words, describe what's going on. Using your imagination, tell what you think each of the two sisters was like. How would each of them approach your daily routine at home? What do you think Jesus meant by the "one thing" he mentions in verse 42?

3. Read Titus 2:3-5. If you are an "older woman," what is your role, according to this passage? What are some ways you can fulfill this in your church or community? If you are a "younger woman," what is expected of you? Take the teaching of this passage and list ways you can fulfill it in your home.

4. Choosing "what is better," as Jesus mentions in Luke 10:42, results in a balanced life. Read the following scriptures, and note what is included in a balanced life: Zechariah 4:6; Matthew 6:25-34; Galatians 5:1,6,13; Philippians 4:6-7; Colossians 3:1-2; 1 Thessalonians 1:2-3; 5:16-18; Hebrews 4:9-11; James 1:5.

~

"It isn't that the doing doesn't need doing, it's that the being must come first, and then we will find that the necessary part of the doing will get done!"

—JILL BRISCOE, *Women's Devotional Bible*

Chapter 21

Moms Are Specal,
Moms Are Nise

Her children arise and call her blessed.

PROVERBS 31:28

How depressing, I thought as I read my next Virtue-producing scripture. I can't remember my children ever arising and calling me blessed. On the contrary, upon arising, they usually call me Mother (pronounced "Muh-therrrrr") and usually at the top of their lungs (as in, "Muh-therrrrr, will you puhleez tell your other daughter to get out of the bathroom?") or in a high-pitched whine (as in, "Muh-therrrrr, I know you haven't even clipped the tags and last time I borrowed something I splattered mustard on it, and you know if I had a job I'd pay you back, but I absolutely NEED to wear your new white sweater to school today. Please-please-please-please-pleeeeese?").

I needed a Plan. Somehow, I had to get Alison and Laura to rise up and call me blessed without my actually asking them. No easy feat, considering their single-minded goal in life was not to call me blessed but to drive me crazy.

Perhaps you think I'm exaggerating? Well, let me tell you about Alison, for example. When she was one, she collected roly-poly bugs in her diaper and ate the knobs off the stereo. At age two she emptied a feather pillow out on the wet lawn, licked the shoe polish off her dad's freshly polished combat boots, and sneaked out of bed one night to "borrow some candy" from the neighbors.

When she was three, I found her hiding in a closet with a pair of scissors in one hand—and her brown curls in the other. Also at three, she ate soap, drank a bottle of clam juice, and stuffed a grape up her nose.

By the time she was four, she had advanced to the "helping" stage. She helped me by washing my seven-dollar blush compact out with soap and water, dumping half a bottle of liquid dish soap in the dishwasher and turning it on, sticking one hundred pushpins in her bedroom wall, and writing her name on her bedspread in lipstick. When she was four and a half, I suggested she go help Daddy.

Age five brought the snail condo in the living room. After being cooped up together for three rainy days, I sent her outside at the first sign of sunshine with a cardboard box and an old spoon for one of her favorite activities, "escargot hunting." An hour or so later she'd collected a boxful, given them all names, conducted marriages, baptisms, and funerals, then during the three seconds when I wasn't watching, dragged them inside the house. Normally I notice things like a boxful of snails on my new gray carpeting, but that day I was busy packing for a weekend trip to my sister's and missed it completely.

I didn't miss it when we arrived home late Sunday night. The escargots had escaped from their box and had left slime trails on the furniture, up the walls, and down the hall. We found snails in the cat food box, in the teacups, between sofa cushions, and inside lampshades. Not a pleasant sight. Or smell.

Age six brought fresh reinforcements to the battle against Mom's wits—Daughter Number Two. Laura came into the world with a twinkle in her eye and a water pistol hidden behind her back.

With Laura, everything is an adventure. A messy adventure. Take the time she conducted the Joys of Food Coloring Adventure. Please don't misunderstand; I'm glad I have an inquisitive child who's always asking, "What would happen if…?" However, I'm less than glad about the results of her inquisitiveness, namely blue mayonnaise, green milk, purple applesauce, and rainbow ricotta cheese.

Laura's the child who, when she couldn't find her shoes, stuck her feet into two loaves of French bread and walked around the house in her "loafers." She's the one who, when she got lost at the mall, told the security officer, "My mom left me here so she could join the circus." The one who, in third grade, wrote and read out loud at a parents' tea, "When I was one, I'd just begun. When I was two, I loved you. When I was three, I coughed up a hairball."

It doesn't matter that she's eleven now and Alison's a senior in high school. I've discovered that children don't outgrow their knack for driving Mom crazy. It seems the taller they get, the more creative they become. We've merely traded grilled cheese sandwiches in the VCR and permanent red marker on the cat's white paws for clothesline gymnastics and ceiling-fan baseball.

Now that they're older, their foolishness is more sophisticated. When they were little, if one wrapped the other one in double-sided tape and smeared her with honey, it was just for the sake of doing it. Now it's justified as "turning her into a human No-Pest strip for a science experiment." Either way, I'm left with honey all over the counter and an empty roll of tape.

And now to complete this portion of my Quest for Virtue, I had to find some way to focus their attention away from their driving-me-crazyness and onto their calling-me-blessedness. But how? What would the VW do?

I opened my Bible to see if any sort of cryptic message would leap out from Proverbs, but alas none did.

Mrs. P., how did you do it? How did you get your kids to stop thinking of you as a target and start seeing you as a real, live person? Was it volunteering to make 150 Frosty the Snowman marshmallow men for the fourth-grade holiday tea even though marshmallows make you gag? Or standing underneath the oak tree—in the rain—trying to coax a scared stray cat down from a top branch because your kindergartner's tears broke your heart?

Did you pick out all the mushrooms in the turkey noodle casserole for your eight-year-old and get out of bed at 11 P.M. to go to the store for the poster board your fifteen-year-old needed to finish a science project? Is that why they called you blessed?

Since both girls were at school, I had a few hours to put my Plan in gear. That is, after I devised one. I looked at the clock—only five hours to plan and execute Operation Call Me Blessed.

First (with the help of a backhoe and a bulldozer), I cleaned their rooms—threw out all the little bits of paper, alphabetized their CDs, hung up their clothes, disinfected their gym shoes. If it moved, I swatted it; if it stayed still, I dusted it.

I worked in their rooms all day, confident I'd be hearing, "Blessed are you, O Mom!" by day's end. When I'd finished, you could actually walk through each room without having to blaze a trail or step on an animal, vegetable, or mineral (or anything else that squished, broke, or left a permanent stain).

Next I scraped together an after-school snack of graham crackers and a half carton of blueberry yogurt.

Minutes before the bus's arrival, I taped up an eight-foot banner that read, "ALISON AND LAURA ARE THE WORLD'S BEST KIDS." Then I perched myself on the living room couch and waited for the blessing to begin.

Laura was first. "I can't believe you did that!" she spewed as she crashed through the front door. Not quite the response I'd expected, but typical, I supposed, of a middle schooler. Alison, I reasoned, would be more appreciative.

Or maybe not. She came in behind Laura, stewing as well as spewing. "Mom, how could you? Everybody saw." They each stomped past me and my open mouth, then halted at their bedroom doors.

Here it comes. Here's where I get my blessing, I thought. The girls rose up. Their eyes grew wide. Their mouths opened. They called me, "Muh-ther-rrrr." As in, "Muh-therrrr, how could you?"

"I didn't mean to upset you girls. Honest," I told them. "I just wanted to… Well, never mind."

I couldn't let them in on my Plan. You know how it is. Forced blessedness doesn't count.

By dinnertime, I was convinced I'd never reach Virtuedom because my children would never, ever rise up and called me blessed. Especially not after I'd embarrassed them in front of the other kids on their bus and disturbed their meticulously cluttered rooms. And the leftover tamale pie and canned pears I'd planned for dinner would do little to help my cause.

As I scraped cold, coagulated fat off the top of the tamale pie, I considered the possibility that the girls have called me blessed without actually saying the words. Like the homemade Mother's Day card from seven-year-old Alison that read:

> *Moms are special*
> *Moms are nise*
> *Moms take care fo you*
> *And I like Moms.*

Or the note that six-year-old Laura slipped under my door that said: "Dear Mom, thakx for all of the thigs yo do." I'd failed to see the love in their chocolate hugs and grape jelly kisses or the ease with which they bring their friends home to meet me.

Yes, they raid my closet, argue for hours over who gets to sit in the front seat or who's better at Playstation games, and "forget" to do their chores (yet never forget a promise I make).

At the same time, they laugh at my jokes, tell me I look good in my bathing suit, suffer through the meals I serve, and occasionally leave some shampoo in the bottle.

By the time I'd opened the canned pears and called everyone to the table, I knew I'd achieved the next level of Total Virtue. I'd been wrong to think they were out to get me, to drive me insane. I'd also been wrong to think I had to plot to get their blessing. They'd been blessing me all along.

Once everyone had taken their seats and commented on the less-than-gourmet meal—and the girls had moaned to Barry about how I'd totally humiliated them and violated their personal space—I stood up.

"Family, I have an announcement to make," I said. "I know I blunder, and I've been known to go off the deep end on a few occasions, but I want to tell you all that I consider myself blessed to be the mom of this family."

The girls dropped their eyes, and Barry smiled. Then Alison and Laura stood up. "Mom," began Alison, "we're glad you're our mom too.

"Now can we order a pizza?"

"You're Such a Mom"

According to my daughters, I'm "*such* a mom." The way they say it, I'm not always sure that's a good thing. They say it when I hover over them, asking questions about their lives or their homework. They say it when I begin a sentence with, "Well, *God* says…" They say it when I laugh at a request for yet another cat or dog.

I'm sure they say it at other times under their breath when I'm acting momlike instead of friendlike. Or when I blow it and make a bad parenting decision. I can't count the times I've heard, "Why can't you be like so-and-so's mom?"

Such comments used to bring me to tears, to make me feel unsure and insecure. *Maybe I'm not a good mom. Maybe I'm doing it all wrong and my girls will turn out...like ME.* I used to worry and wonder if they wouldn't be better off with some other mother. Someone who knew what she was doing. Someone who didn't feel she was "winging it."

But then I realized none of us knows what we're doing all the time. Every mom I know is basically winging it. None of us had ever been mothers before we became mothers; it's pretty much a learn-as-you-go occupation. We might not ever feel as if we know what we're doing, but we can be certain that the children we've been given are gifts from the hands and heart of a Father who always knows what he's doing. That means, with all my faults and weaknesses, I am a perfect fit (not a perfect parent) as my daughters' mother. He chose them for me and vice versa.

I may be *such* a mom and I may make tons of mistakes, but I'm the mom God knew they needed. I just pray that when they have children of their own, they'll remember that they, too, are a perfect fit and that when they're called *such* a mom, they'll hear it not as an insult but as a blessing.

Digging Deeper

1. What are some memories of your own mother? In what ways are you like her? In what ways are you different?

2. Proverbs 22:6 says, "Train a child in the way he should go, and when he is old he will not turn from it." What is "the way" a child should go? (See Deuteronomy 6; John 3:5-18; 14:5-7; Ephesians 2:8-9; also Matthew 19:14.)

3. The Bible gives ample warnings to parents about *not* training their children. Read the following, and write down what you learn: 1 Samuel 2:12-36; Proverbs 10:17; 22:15; 23:13-14; 29:15.

4. We want to be good mothers, but we often worry about whether we're doing a good job. Read the following Bible passages, then

note how you can apply them to parenting your own children: Psalm 139:15-16; Luke 2:41-52; Ephesians 6:1-4; Hebrews 12:5-13; Deuteronomy 4:5-10; Matthew 19:13-15.

"When children become adults, they remember the little things you did together, like playing ball, roasting marshmallows, or hiking a trail. They rarely remember toys."

—from *Wit and Wisdom for Women*

Chapter 22

What, Me Noble?

Many women do noble things,
but you surpass them all.

PROVERBS 31:29

Blond, beautiful, and better than me. At least that's what I thought
when *She* moved into the neighborhood. I discovered my hunches
were correct shortly after the moving van left her driveway.

Ding dong, rang my doorbell. Standing on my doorstep, sporting crisp
white shorts below a crisper white shirt and bearing the crispiest-looking
peanut butter cookies I'd ever seen, was my new neighbor. She greeted me
with a smile.

"Hi!" the woman said, only it sounded more like "hey" in her slow,
Southern drawl. "I'm Claire Barnett, and we jus' moved in down the street.
Goodness, what with unpackin' all our things, gettin' the boys signed up
for school this morning, and deliverin' cookies to the neighbors, I barely
had time to take Mama to the doctor." She smiled again and held out her
well-manicured hand. "And you are?"

I looked down at my worn-out jeans and baggy T-shirt and, after wip-
ing it off on my pant leg, offered her my raggedy-nailed hand. "Nancy.
Kennedy. Hi," I stammered as I accepted her welcome-to-the-neighborhood
gift (which I should have been offering to her).

That's what a Woman of Noble Character would do, I scolded myself.

When was the last time you took homemade cookies to a neighbor? Forget that... When was the last time you even baked homemade cookies? Not in this decade, dear. Looks like this Claire person has you whipped in the noble deeds department, hands down.

"Would you like to come in?" I eventually asked. It wasn't that I didn't want her in my house; I just prefer a week's notice before somebody pops by unexpectedly.

"I'd love to," she said, stepping delicately inside (and stepping even more delicately over Laura's pile of spilled glitter in the dining room, which I hadn't gotten around to vacuuming). I shoved my pile of papers off one end of the table and invited her to join me for a cup of coffee.

"I hope you don't mind, but I brought some with me," she drawled as she pulled a tin of my favorite French vanilla flavored coffee out of her purse. "All we need is a little water, and we're all set for a nice gettin' acquainted chat."

When she didn't pull a couple of mugs and a gallon of milk out of her purse, I rustled up a couple of leftover McDonald's napkins, washed out two dirty cups from the counter, and poured the last dribble of milk into a plastic cup. Then I considered bolting out the door.

A Woman of Noble Character is clothed with strength and dignity, I reminded myself. *She laughs at the future. She doesn't hide from her neighbors.*

After I'd gone back in and sat down with Claire, we did what women always do—we gabbed about the usual things: Where are you from? How many kids do you have? What does your husband do? Do you belong to a church? Who does your hair? How noble are you?

Of course, Claire didn't ask me that, nor did I ask her...exactly. I merely fished around, tossing out casual queries: Have you ever traveled to California for grasshopper pie? How are your biceps? What are your views on the color purple? How many times have your children risen up and called you blessed?

She didn't say it in so many words, but from her gentle quietness and all-around sweet spirit, I could tell she fulfilled the qualifications of a Virtuous Woman—and was, without a doubt, the Most Noble woman I had ever met. If I didn't like her so much, I would've hated her.

After she graciously answered all my questions, she brushed the crumbs from the table, carried the dishes into the kitchen, unstopped my clogged drain, and tidied up my bathroom. Before she could offer to rotate my tires, I thanked her for coming over, escorted her out the door, then sat down and fumed.

How dare she be so noble! The nerve of that woman! After all these months of sacrifice and self-denial in the Search for Virtue, she moves in and steals it away from me! Well, if she can be a Woman of Noble Character, then I'll just be nobler.

I set out on my Be More Noble Than Claire campaign that very day. I loaded my purse with flavored coffee—and tossed in a few linen napkins and a jar of nondairy creamer. I practiced stepping delicately. I brushed my teeth and my hair. Even so, after a few days I didn't feel any nobler. I decided to take a walk for inspiration.

As I just happened to walk past Claire's house, I spied her out in her yard, looking crisp while weeding a patch for a garden. She waved and started to dust herself off to say hello, but I gestured for her to continue her gardening (making a mental note to dig up my dying rhododendrons and plant plastic geraniums in the front window box).

"Come back later for some homemade peach cobbler!" she called.

"I'd love to!" I replied, flashing a smile bigger and brighter than hers. It had faded by the time I got home. *Peach cobbler!* I fumed as I opened cans of sliced peaches and slammed cupboard doors looking for flour and sugar. *This woman is definitely getting on my nerves.*

That afternoon when the girls came in from school (and I'd greeted them with my own hot peach cobbler and ice cream), I tried involving them in a little neighborly getting-acquainted activity. "Girls, we have new neighbors. I want you two to go over and introduce yourselves, then come back here and tell me everything you find. I want details: what books she has on her shelves, if there's dust on the top of her fridge—everything."

"Muh-therrrrr!" they cried at the same time. Then as Laura put her dish in the sink, Alison scolded me. "We'll go over and meet her, but we're not going to spy for you!"

"Never mind then. I'll go myself." After I polished my nails, spray starched and ironed my T-shirt, and stuffed a box of donuts in my purse, I marched over to her house with Noble Intentions. Claire met me at the door with a glass of iced tea in one hand and a tube of caulking in the other.

"I was jus' caulkin' the tub when I saw you comin' up the street, so I quickly fixed you some tea," she said, handing it to me. "I think it's vital for a woman to know how to do minor repairs around the house, don't you? You know, check her own oil, rewire a lamp, properly solvent-cement a pipe joint under the bathroom sink."

"I couldn't agree more," I said, not having a clue about pipe joints. "When my pipe joints aren't properly solvent-cemented, well, it just ruins my whole day."

As I rambled on about things I knew nothing about, I stole a few glances around her house and took inventory: alphabetized spices in her spice rack, no piles of laundry stacked on chairs—she didn't even have unpacked moving boxes sitting in her hallway. And her peach cobbler was the best I'd ever tasted.

I had to get out of there. Her noble character was about to make me do something I knew I'd regret.

"I can do origami!" I blurted on my way out the door.

"Really? You know, I've been wantin' to learn that ever since I was little." She smiled that perfect-toothed smile of hers. "Do you think you could teach me sometime?"

How could I refuse? That wouldn't be noble of me. "Anytime you want, you just let me know."

Later that night I couldn't sleep. I sat in bed with a pile of paper, trying—unsuccessfully—to turn at least one piece into a bird.

"Why are you so obsessed with this neighbor?" asked Barry, watching me frustrate myself into a snit.

"I'm not obsessed!" I hissed, then wadded up another origami goof and hurled it to join the dozen or so wads already on the floor. "If you must know, it's because she's nobler than me. She can do everything, Barry. She chauffeurs senior citizens to the market—and I'll bet she even cleans behind her stove."

"Nancy, you're being ridiculous." He took the origami book out of my hand and set it on the floor. "You're noble enough, and besides, where does it say there can't be more than one Woman of Noble Character?"

"Noble *enough?* Thanks a lot." I opened my Bible and showed him Proverbs 31. "See here? It says, 'Many women do noble things, but you surpass them all.' I'm supposed to be noblest. I can't do that as long as she's around."

Since I couldn't sleep—and couldn't make my paper look like a bird— I climbed out of bed and grabbed a tube of caulking. As I searched the bathroom for holes to patch, I determined to step up my Outdo Claire campaign.

However, as the weeks rolled by and I discovered that I couldn't keep up with her, let alone outdo her, my philosophy changed from "Anything she can do, I can do better" to "Duck whenever I see her coming, don't answer the door, and especially don't return her phone messages asking about origami lessons."

Unfortunately, the more out of sight I tried to keep, the less out of mind she became. In fact, she was all I thought about. And the more I thought about her, the less noble I felt. Not only that, I knew I needed to go and reconcile with her.

"But I didn't do anything wrong!" I whined to the Lord.

Are you envious? Did you try to make yourself out to be something you're not? Did you lie?

"I just want to be noble!" I protested.

Then do the noble thing and make peace with your neighbor. She's done nothing wrong.

I conceded and agreed to do it the next day.

The next day came, and with it came (Can you believe it? She beat me to it!) Claire on my doorstep, standing with her sweet smile and a basket of blueberry muffins.

"Have I offended you?" she asked.

"No!" I said and ushered her over to the couch. "You haven't offended me, but I'm afraid I've offended you." She tilted her head, looking puzzled, so I brought out my Bible and showed her the Proverbs 31 passage. Then I filled her in on everything—my vows to attain Virtue, my successes, my failures—and especially my attempt to beat her at being Most Noble.

"But I'm not noble!" she protested as she read over the passage. She handed my Bible back to me and shook her head. "And I'm not virtuous— I know I can't do all this. I'd be afraid to even try. You're the noble one— and awfully brave to take this on all by yourself."

I laughed. "I'm not brave, but that's what I thought at first too—that it would take will power and bravery and everything I had within me to achieve Virtue. But then I got to know the VW (that's what I call her). I found out that, although she did some pretty incredible things—I mean, I never knew anybody who planted vineyards in their spare time—in many ways, she was just like me. She fed her family, she made beds and cared for her children—and the Bible calls her noble. But it wasn't the things she did that made her noble; she did noble things because of who she was—a woman of faith in almighty God."

Claire patted my hands. "If you truly believe that, why are you tryin' so hard to be noble?"

I lowered my head and admitted, "Pride."

I'd tried to be noble by my own efforts, just as I'd tried to attain Virtue on my own. The irony is, in striving to find Virtue, I only find failure. But in my failure, when I turn to the Lord and acknowledge my utter helplessness, he picks me up, and I find grace. Then as I walk in grace, letting God's Spirit work in and through me, I find the Virtue I so desperately desire. It's Christ in me, the hope of glory (Colossians 1:27).

Claire sat and listened, then we broke out our favorite coffees to "celebrate the moments of our lives."

"So what you're sayin' is, I can be a Woman of Noble Character too?" she asked as she stirred her coffee.

"If you're in Christ, my friend, then you already are."

She hesitated, then smiled. "I have one last question: Does this mean no origami lesson?"

How to Be Noble

An ancient Greek proverb says, "If you wish to be good, first believe that you are bad." The problem is, although we come to Christ initially because we believe we are bad, it doesn't take long to forget. That's when we start trying to be good. We work at being noble and virtuous. We might even fool ourselves into thinking we can be noble, good, and righteous by trying. However, even our best deeds, if done to earn favor with God, are nothing more than dirty rags in his sight (Isaiah 64:6).

Martin Luther knew about the sin of trying to be good. As a sixteenth-century Catholic priest in Germany, Luther diligently and desperately spent hours in prayer and self-flagellation, trying to be acceptable to God. If the Lord gave grades for effort, Luther would have gotten straight A's.

But even his most fervent attempts couldn't produce goodness, and his efforts only drove him to despair. It wasn't until he grasped the truth of the gospel—"The just shall live by faith" (Romans 1:17, KJV)—that he began preaching the radical message of grace.

Do you want to be noble? Then stop trying. Instead, believe that you are not noble, that you're not good and never will be, no matter how hard you try. It's Christ's goodness, his noble character, that produces noble character in us.

His effort, his work, his goodness…my gain.

Digging Deeper

1. Describe the qualities of a "woman of noble character."

2. Although "goodness" is a noble goal for a Christian, why would God be offended by our noble efforts to be good apart from him? (See Galatians 1:1-9; 3:1-5; 4:8-10.)

3. Colossians 1:27 says Christ in us is the hope of glory. What does it mean to have Christ *in* us? (See John 1:12-13; Romans 8:9-11,15-17.) Read the following scriptures: 1 Corinthians 1:28-30; 2 Corinthians 3:13-15; 5:17-20; Galatians 3:28; Ephesians 1:2-4; 2:12-14; 4:32; Philippians 3:8-9. What does it mean to be *in Christ?*

4. Read Colossians 1. Contrast a life outside of Christ with a life in Christ. What fruit will be evident in the life of someone secure in Christ? For example, one of the first changes I noticed after becoming a Christian was a love for going to church. No longer alienated from God (verse 21), I wanted to be in his presence and with his people. What fruit can you identify in your own life that can be attributed only to God's goodness working in you?

"*We soon find it all but impossible to live the Christian life with our own strength and goodness. It is through God's strength that we know courage, and through his power that we know goodness. When we realize this, surrender becomes our priority.*"

—JUDITH LECHMAN, *Women's Devotional Bible*

Chapter 23

Beauty: It's NOT a Pretty Thing

Charm is deceptive, and beauty is fleeting.
PROVERBS 31:30

One assumes that to know for oneself that "charm is deceptive and beauty is fleeting," one must be charming and beautiful to begin with. Unfortunately, I am one who is not. I mean, I don't cause kids to point and dogs to bark, and my husband doesn't put a bag over my head when we go out in public (although I've been tempted to do it myself once or twice). It's just that, the older I get, the more I look like my Uncle Burt—mustache and all. And then I think, God made me exactly this way. Obviously, we have a Creator with a sense of humor.

"What other explanation could there be for facial hair?" I said to my reflection in the mirror. To the rescue, a box of Mustache No More wax hair remover, promising me a smooth, hair-free upper lip with a minimum of discomfort. A mere gentle tugging sensation.

Although I knew beauty was in the eye of the beholder and only skin deep, I still wanted to experience it—if only for a fleeting moment. In fact, I'd convinced myself that in order to truly understand the deception of charm and the fleeting property of beauty, I must do all that I could to attain them.

With the cry, "In the name of all that's Virtuous!" I placed the block of wax in a saucepan on the stove, let it melt, then smeared the warm wax on my "mustache" with a Popsicle stick.

So far, so good, I thought, until a few seconds later when, with cooled and hardened wax on my skin, I reached the point of no return: the gentle tugging sensation. That's when I discovered THE most sensitive area on the human body is the upper lip.

I took hold of one end of the hardened wax and gave myself the same pep talk I give my kids when ripping off a Band-Aid. "One quick ZIP! and it's all over."

I answered myself with their usual whining reply, "No! It's gonna hurt! I don't want to be brave!"

But I had no choice, unless I wanted to walk around with hardened wax on my face. R-r-r-i-i-p-p-p! It felt as if every hair had been connected to a nerve that ran from deep inside my nose all the way into my ears. It brought tears to my eyes and a scream to my lips.

My nose ran, and my lip swelled and remained bright red for an hour and a half. But as promised, my upper lip appeared wonderfully smooth and hair-free. At least until the following week when it would be cryin' time again.

Once I de-mustached, I turned my attention to another hairy sub-ject—my legs. You see, I was blessed with thick, lustrous brown hair—none of it, however, on my head.

Recently I bought an epilator. The commercial showed a woman gen-tly and painlessly gliding an electric shaverlike device over her legs. Voilà! With a gentle tugging sensation, each individual hair is eased out. Legs are left silky smooth for up to six weeks.

"Gentle tugging sensation" should've been a red flag for me, but in my frenzy to find a hairless existence, all I heard was "six weeks." That's only 8.7 times a year I'd have to bother with the whole hairy ordeal.

The commercial failed to mention a couple of things. For instance, initially it takes about five hours to get all the hair off. Five hours of my life that could've been spent feeding the hungry, praying for world peace, or even cleaning the mildew off the shower window sill—those hours I spent removing hair from my legs.

For conscience-easing's sake, I didn't do it all at once. It was more like a half-hour here, a half-hour there. Besides, that's about all the "gentle tugging sensation" I could bear at one time.

The commercial also failed to mention the red, measlelike blotches that the "gentle tugging" causes. Raised, itchy blotches that last for hours and hours and cause strangers to avoid you when they see you in the market.

Now if epilating really lasted six weeks, I could live with five hours of pain and another three or four of blotches 8.7 times a year. However, the commercial only promised UP TO six weeks. That's for the semihairless to begin with, NOT for those of us who started braiding our leg hair at age nine. I'm lucky if I can go one week hair-, and therefore care-, free.

I hate to admit this, but my search for fleeting beauty didn't stop at hair removal. The truth is, I tried everything I could over the course of two beauty-intense months: shoving my corn-throbbing feet into tight high heels, having my face chemically peeled and my body whipped with seaweed. I permed, moussed, gelled, frosted, streaked, and colored my hair: ash blond, chestnut brown, mahogany red—and for three horrifying hours—pumpkin orange. I soaked in an Authentic Ancient Egyptian mud bath and baked my skin to a crisp golden brown while lying in a coffinlike box under ultraviolet lights.

I still ended up looking like Uncle Burt.

Eventually I decided my daily facial program and weekly deep-cleansing and rejuvenating programs weren't enough. So one day I scheduled an entire day for serious beauty Rx…

As I sat on the edge of my bathtub, I watched the sudsing, foaming milk beads turn the water a pearlescent color. With Navajo Adobe Clay Moisturizing Masque on my face, hot wax on my upper lip, a raw egg pack on my hair, and my legs red, blotchy, and itchy from epilating, I eased myself into my bubble bath and snuggled deep into my bubbly paradise. No distractions, no worries, no cares. Just peace and—

"Uh, Mom?" Alison poked her head into the bathroom. "That was Dad on the phone. He said to be ready in twenty minutes because his boss is taking you two out to dinner."

Jolted out of the serenity of my tub and into the bedlam of reality, I panicked. Tonight? That couldn't be! Twenty minutes? Impossible. Couldn't be done. No way.

"Okay, Nancy, don't panic," I coached myself. "Just take a deep breath. You can do it."

I took a breath. "Aaaaahhh!"

I took another breath and asked Alison to get out my raspberry-colored knit dress and black pumps from my closet. Then, turning on the water, I jumped into the shower, zipped the wax off my lip, and washed the clay facial masque down the drain.

Piece of cake, I thought as I stuck my raw eggy hair under the shower. The HOT shower.

A word of advice: When using raw egg as a hair conditioner, ALWAYS use cool water to rinse it out.

"What's that smell?" I sniffed. "Alison, are you cooking eggs—" I stopped short and slowly patted my head. I was the one cooking eggs. In my hair.

"Fifteen minutes, Mom!" Alison yelled.

I started pulling egg out of my hair as fast as I could, yelling for help. Alison burst through the door. "Mom!" she said. "Do you know you have scrambled egg in your hair?"

"Yes, I do—and I can't get it out!"

With twelve minutes left, I prayed. "Lord? Can you help me please?"

"Hey, Mom—I have an idea," Alison said, handing me a towel. "Just dry your hair any old way."

"And look like a scarecrow? I don't call that a good idea."

"Don't worry, Mom. It'll be fine. Just dry off and get dressed."

"I don't know, Alison." I shrugged my shoulders. "But I don't know what else to do. Just go get me some stockings."

A moment later Alison came back into the bathroom holding up my only pair of pantyhose tied in a perfect double half-hitch knot. "Uh, Mom? I think maybe someone's been practicing knot tying."

I checked the clock to see if I had time to panic. Nope, I had ten minutes left, and I needed at least fifteen for a panic attack. I did it anyway.

"I can't go out looking like this," I wailed. "I look awful. When Dad comes home, tell him I'm not here."

"Mom, I can't lie for you! Besides, who cares what you look like?"

"I care." I slumped to the edge of the bathtub. "I can't go, and that's that."

"You have to go, Mom. Anyway, what do you always tell me when I say I can't go to school because I hate the way I look?"

"Wear a hat?"

"Well, yeah, but you always say stuff like, 'Pretty is as pretty does' and 'What's inside is more important than what's on the outside.' And your favorite, 'Real beauty is a gentle and quiet spirit, which is of great worth in God's sight.' Then you usually start singing, 'This little light of mine…'"

Since when did she start paying attention to me?

"Fine," I answered her, "if you want to get biblical, what about Queen Esther? She spent a whole year making herself beautiful."

"Yeah, but she did it to save the entire Jewish nation. You're just going out to dinner."

As much as I hated to admit it, she was right.

"All right, I'll go. But I'm not going looking like this." I pulled my dress over my head and decided to go barelegged—that is until I noticed the red blotches all over my legs. I'd forgotten that I'd just used the epilator. At least the spots matched the color of my dress. "Do you think they'll believe I'm wearing polka-dotted hose?"

"Mom, get real," Alison answered. She rummaged through my makeup bag and handed me a jar. "Here. Try putting some of this makeup on your legs. Didn't you tell me girls used to do that in high school instead of wearing stockings?"

She started smearing makeup on one of my legs, and I worked on the other. When we finished applying the makeup to my legs, we put the remainder on my face. A brush of blush, a whisk of mascara, a dab of eye shadow, and—ta-da! A perfectly made-up face. My hair, however, was still a mop of dried-out egg. I cried as I struggled to pull a comb through it.

Alison handed me a long, silky blue scarf. "Here, Mom, we'll take this scarf like so," she said, winding it turban-style around my head. "Then we'll just tuck it in like this." She handed me my big silver hoop earrings and slipped a few silver bangle bracelets on my wrist. "Now look."

I stepped back and looked in the mirror. It wasn't a look I'd normally go for, and I smelled like an Egg McMuffin, but I didn't have a choice. Whatever inner beauty I possessed would have to be sufficient. I grabbed a pair of blue sandals from under the bed and ran outside just as Barry pulled up in the driveway.

"What's with the headpiece?" Barry whispered, raising one eyebrow.

"Don't ask. PLEASE don't ask," I said, climbing into the backseat of the car.

Mr. Rollins, Barry's boss, turned around from the front seat, introduced himself, and sniffed the air. "Say, Barry," he said, "if you don't mind, let's forget about the steakhouse tonight. I just had a sudden yen for an omelet."

On the way to the restaurant, my head started to itch from the scarf, and I knew I had to take it off, dried egg or no dried egg.

"This is really embarrassing," I squeaked, "and you can pretend you don't even know me, but I have to take this thing off my head."

As I did, I explained the whole story, apologized profusely, then spent the rest of the ride brushing out my hair. By the time we arrived, I discovered I hadn't died of embarrassment, and Barry and Mr. Rollins were still willing to be seen with me. Also, I was able to brush the egg out, merely ending up with flat hair. It's not the most flattering hairstyle on me, but at least it beat the scarf that made my head itch. Besides, I couldn't juggle scratching my head and my itchy legs at the same time.

Not only did I survive dinner that night, I actually had a good time. I even liked Barry's referring to me as his "egghead wife."

Later, over coffee and cheesecake, I chanced to overhear Mr. Rollins tell Barry, "Your wife is lovely, Kennedy."

I just smiled and scratched my leg.

Lasting Beauty

I've always wished I could wake up looking like Cindy Crawford, and it finally happened last Christmas—sort of. A friend sent me a card with a photo of my body and Cindy's face. For me it was an improvement; for Cindy… Well, she could stand to lose fifteen pounds.

I often think that what I really need is a month of intensive beauty spa treatment, but that won't result in lasting change. External beauty is fleeting. However, there is a beauty that endures, although it's both costly and painful.

Real beauty comes in a two-step process. The apostle Paul described the first step when he wrote, "We are hard pressed on every side, but not crushed; perplexed, but not in despair; persecuted, but not abandoned; struck down, but not destroyed.… Though outwardly we are wasting away, yet inwardly we are being renewed day by day. For our light and momentary troubles are achieving for us an eternal glory that far outweighs them all" (2 Corinthians 4:8-9,16-17).

Step one is the purifying effect of the pain and sorrow in our lives—

relationship woes and sickness, financial calamities and depression. These things strip us of our own beauty and prepare us for step two, which brings the reflected glory of God in our lives as he continually transforms us into his likeness.

The truth is, I could have perfect features and be pretty but still not be beautiful. On the other hand, when God's beauty shines through my own quirky features, *I am beautiful.*

Digging Deeper

1. Proverbs 31:30 says, "Charm is deceptive, and beauty is fleeting." How would you define "charm"? How is it deceptive? What steps have you taken in your pursuit of charm and beauty?

2. List your best features. Psalm 139:14 says, "I praise you because I am fearfully and wonderfully made." What does Psalm 45:11 say about how the Lord sees you? Write a prayer of praise and thanksgiving for the unique way God has created you.

3. In our society, appearance is everything. But where does the Lord look for beauty? Read the following passages and record what you learn: 1 Samuel 16:7; Mark 14:3-9; 1 Peter 3:3-5.

4. Numerous times throughout the Bible we're told to "fear the Lord," and the last part of Proverbs 31:30 says, "A woman who fears the LORD is to be praised." But rather than tremble in terror before him, God invites us, his children, to "approach [his] throne of grace with confidence, so that we may receive mercy and find grace" (Hebrews 4:16). Using a concordance, look up the phrase "the fear of the Lord." Some modern translations use the words *reverence* or *honor* in place of *fear.* With that in mind, what does it mean for a woman to "fear the Lord"? How would that bring praise to her? In what ways do you fear the Lord?

"Character contributes to beauty. It fortifies a woman as her youth fades. A mode of conduct, a standard of courage, discipline, fortitude, and integrity can do a great deal to make a woman beautiful."

—JACQUELINE BISSET, *Values and Virtues*

Chapter 24

And the Winner Is…

Give her the reward she has earned.

PROVERBS 31:31

I t had been a grueling, self-sacrificing, often-humiliating and humbling, sometimes-victorious ordeal, but I'd FINALLY reached the end—the last verse in my Search for Total Virtuization. I gathered the family together in the living room to share my news. "Family," I said with my open Bible in hand, "standing before you is an almost-Virtuous Woman." I waited for accolades but received only yawns.

"That's nice, Mom," said Alison, getting up to leave.

"Way to go," said Barry as he leafed through the stack of week-old newspapers on the floor.

"Can I go to the Roller Barn?" asked Laura.

"You people don't understand!" I cried, pulling Alison back into the room and swatting the newspaper away from Barry. "For the past year I've toiled and put myself—and you—through the most burdensome tasks and situations." I paused for dramatic effect, striking my Famous Hollywood Actress Winning the Academy Award pose. "And now, I've come to the end of my Journey."

No one appeared impressed.

The girls offered ho-hum "way-to-go-Moms," and Barry went back to reading the paper. "Tell us when you get there," he said from behind the business page.

Undaunted (I'd grown accustomed to their unresponsiveness concerning my Pursuit), I readied myself for my Reward (à la verse 31). The problem was, unlike my sister Peggy who, when she was eight years old, won a set of Popeye rub-on tattoos as the Holiday Theater's Saturday movie matinee door prize, I've never won anything.

Ed McMahon has never showed up at my door. The Publisher's Clearinghouse people have never surprised me with a zillion dollar cardboard check the size of a refrigerator. I'm never the eighth caller to the radio station—even when I know who put the "bop" in the bop-shu-bop-shu-bop.

However, despite nearly forty years of being a nonwinner, I've remained optimistic, telling myself that somewhere out there is a prize with my name on it and I'M GOING TO FIND IT. I had to. It was the only thing standing in the way of my becoming Virtuous. (How quickly I'd forgotten all I had learned about achieving Virtue.)

In the following weeks, I tried everything. I bought raffle tickets from every Quilt Guild member, Lion's Club Lioness, or high-school band booster who accosted me outside the market. I played Bingo. I played something illegal-sounding called Bunco. I even played the lottery. I won zilch.

Then I turned from games of chance to games of skill: relay races at the church picnic. But when my partner in the three-legged race screamed for an amputation after I veered us into a hedge, and after I accidentally tripped the pastor's wife during the hop-with-a-grapefruit-between-your-knees race, I reconsidered using my physical skills and opted instead to use my mental ones: a radio contest.

To win a thousand dollars, I simply had to be caller number twelve and correctly identify the mystery voice. For days, I sat with the radio on one side of me and the phone on the other. As soon as I heard the disc jockey say, "Call in and win," I'd press my auto-dial button on the phone. In theory, it sounds easy. But in the real world of busy signals and greedy people with nothing better to do than to take my prize away from me, I had trouble getting through.

Still, with my eyes on the prize, I persevered. Every hour, as call-in time neared, I'd scream, "Nobody touch the phone!" and stand, finger poised and ready for action.

After several days of almost nonstop trying (I did take time out to sleep, shower, and toss bologna sandwiches to the family), I finally got through. Not as caller number three or nine or fourteen but as CALLER NUMBER TWELVE!

"Hello, you're caller number twelve," said the disc jockey.

"I'm caller number twelve? I'm caller number twelve! I'm caller number twelve!" I hopped up and down, squealing in anticipation of my prize. "When do I get my prize? Where's my thousand dollars?"

The disc jockey laughed. "Whoa, first give us your name and identify our mystery voice."

I took a deep breath. This was it. I knew the voice—I'd listened to it for days on end. I'd told my kids who it was. I'd told Barry. I'd told the water softener man and the FedEx delivery lady.

I opened my mouth to say, "Art Fleming, the original host of *Jeopardy*," only it came out, "Mushy Callahan."

"I'm sorry, you're incorrect." Then the phone went dead.

"Mushy Callahan?" I couldn't believe I'd said Mushy Callahan. I hadn't even thought about him in years. Actually, I never even knew him. He was just a man in a photo, wearing a cowboy suit and sitting on a horse, a movie actor relative of ours, according to my dad. (But now that I think of it, Dad also used to tell me eating too many green olives would cause hair to grow on my chest.)

I considered trying again the next hour, but I'd given my name and was too embarrassed to call back. Instead, I switched radio stations.

This one called you.

They would choose a number at random, and all you had to do was answer your phone: "Win with WINN, W-I-N-N— Always a hit, never a miss." No mystery voice, no trivia question, no "In ten seconds, give me ten words beginning with the letters PL."

The only catch: You didn't know when they would call, so you had to answer your phone with the WINNing phrase every time it rang. Annoying, sure, but well worth the prize: a vacation for four to New York.

The first time the phone rang, I forgot and said hello, which was a good thing because it was the dentist calling to confirm Laura's cleaning appointment. The next time it rang, I forgot again. That time it was someone wanting to sell me a time-share vacation home.

The third time I remembered. "Win with WINN, W-I-N-N— Always a hit, never a miss."

"I'm sorry, I must have the—Nancy, what are you doing?" (It was Barry.)

"Trying to win a prize."

From the *tsk tsk tsk* on his end of the phone, I could tell he was shaking his head. "I thought you had to identify the mystery voice."

I winced at the thought of my earlier on-air faux pas. "Well…this one's more challenging, more exciting. Besides, they call me."

He paused. "I don't know… What's the prize?"

I told him about the vacation trip to New York. He paused again, then offered to buy me a one-way ticket if I'd go back to answering with a conventional "Hello."

"Barry! You can't buy a prize. You have to win it or earn it." This time I shook my head and *tsk tsk tsk*ed.

"Whatever. Anyway, I just called to tell you that some of the guys in the shop read your last article in the paper, and they wanted you to know they liked it. I told them, 'Everything my wife does is good.' "

"You did?"

"Sure, I'm always bragging about you."

We said good-bye, and immediately the phone rang again.

"Win with WINN, W-I-N-N— Always a hit, never a miss."

"Sweetie? Is that you?" (It was Kathy.)

"Yes, Kathy. I'm trying to win a prize on the radio." I filled her in on all that had happened since the last time we had talked—it had been ages. "All that's left is verse 31, 'Give her the reward she has earned.' After I get that, I'll finally be a Virtuous Woman."

"Oh, sweetie, that's so adorably precious. I knew all along you'd make it." We chit-chatted awhile longer until the call-waiting signal clicked in my ear.

"Gotta go, Kathy!" I said in one breath, then, "Win with WINN, W-I-N-N— Always a hit, never a miss" in another.

"Still me, sweetie."

"Sorry." I clicked again. "Win with WINN, W-I-N-N— Always a hit, never a miss."

"Hello? Is this the Kennedys?" (It was the chairman of the community charity auction.)

I sighed. "Yes. This is Nancy." Then I explained the radio contest.

"Oh. Well, I'm calling to thank you for the quilted wall hanging you donated for our auction last week."

"Oh. Oh? Do I win a prize?"

She hesitated. "No…unless maybe satisfaction for your labor. Or how about the good feeling of knowing you're helping the community?"

"I guess they're okay too," I said, then thanked her and hung up.

The next few days went much the same. Either I forgot to answer with the catch phrase, or it wasn't the radio station calling. Finally I got fed up. One day the phone rang, and I decided I wouldn't answer it. I'd just let it ring. Wouldn't answer it. Wasn't going to embarrass myself one more time. Just let it ring… But when I heard the disc jockey say, "We'll let it ring once more, then try someone else," I pounced on the phone.

"Win with WINN, W-I-N-N— Always a hit, never a miss!" I yelled into the receiver, out of breath from racing across the room.

"Oh, sweetie, are you still trying to win that prize?"

"Kathy," I panted. "Yes." (Pant, pant.) "No." (Pant, pant.) "I don't know." (Pant, pant, pant.)

"Well, if you still are, I called to tell you about a contest down at the mall that's just your cup of tea." She gave me the details, and after scribbling a note to the family, I went off to claim my sure prize.

When I got inside the mall, I stopped short in my tracks. Sitting at the Frequent Shopper booth next to a sign beckoning mall patrons to "Guess How Many?" was a gallon-sized fishbowl filled with M&M's. Anyone who knows me (or has ever heard my answering machine message instructing callers to either "leave your name and number, send a fax, or put M&M's in the mailbox") knows my fondness for the candies. *Yes, Kathy, you're right. This is my cup of tea.*

I spent the rest of the day with pen and paper, doing any and every geometric and algebraic equation I could recall from high school. After several hours I had computed the area of several triangles and the volume of three or four spheres and had even deduced that two trains leaving Podunk on parallel tracks at different rates of speed and an hour apart will meet at 280 kilometers outside of Podunk. However, I could not determine the number of M&M's in that fishbowl.

Dejected, I wrote down a number at random and handed it to the man at the counter. He read it, shook his head as if to say, "Not even close," and bid me, "Have a nice day." Then I went home.

However, somewhere between being wished "Have a nice day" and pulling into my driveway, I had a revelation. As I drove toward the comfort of my family, I realized that I had already received my prize and I hadn't even noticed: Barry boasting about me to his friends, a note in the mail from a friend saying she prays for me daily, people appreciating my work, even my children occasionally arising and calling me blessed.

My real reward in life is satisfaction from my labor, trials that cause me to grow, and a good night's sleep. It's God's peace in the midst of turmoil. It's his mercy in my repentance, his strength in my weakness. It's grace in pain and joy in sorrow. It's a merry heart that does good like medicine (Proverbs 17:22).

Not only that, heaven is waiting for me, where someday I'll see Jesus face to face and hear him call my name, have God himself wipe away my tears and invite me to sit with him upon his throne.

That's my prize! I burst through the front door and danced around the living room while the family looked on.

"Did you win the contest, Mom?" asked Laura as I hugged her.

"No! I lost!" I shouted, still hugging, still dancing.

"Uh-oh, Dad," Laura said, wiggling out from my clutches, "I think Mom's lost more than the contest."

Barry guided me over to the couch. "Are you okay? Want to sit down? Take a bath?"

"You don't understand," I said, kicking off my shoes, flopping down, and leaning my head back in my hands. "I lost the contest, but I got my prize. I've had it all along. It's you—and the girls. It's our home and our friends. It's Jesus."

My family stood and stared at me, then Alison smiled. "Does this mean your Search for Virtue is over, Mom?" she asked.

"Yes, Alison, it is."

And with that, I walked over to my desk, picked out a red pen, and wrote DONE across my list.

And everybody said, *"Amen."*

Our True Reward

Scripture paints a picture of God Almighty coming to earth one day, bringing his reward with him—a reward he plans to give to us. "Say to the Daughter of Zion, 'See, your Savior comes!'" writes the prophet Isaiah. "'See, his reward is with him, and his recompense accompanies him'" (62:11).

A reward is something given for a service or an attainment, and a recompense connotes compensation for something that was lost. Take a moment to think about that. Jesus, the Son of God and the One whom we crucified, is returning to earth with rewards for us, the least deserving.

His recompense accompanies him. Even though we turned our backs on him. We went our own way. We defied his authority and lost our way because of our selfish choice. Yet he's coming back with rewards and with recompense. Prizes, gifts, goodies, and crowns. For those who are in Christ, we'll get the privilege of being rulers and honored guests at the Father's table. Coheirs with Jesus. Forever and ever.

Even though this is a glorious thought, I often lose sight of this truth. My mind is most often preoccupied with everyday stuff. Eternity seems such a long way off. Sometimes it doesn't even seem real. But then I'll be outside, and a gentle breeze will blow across my face, and I'll remember that the Holy Spirit is like the wind. Or I'll hear a baby cry, and I'll feel a helplessness, a longing for Home. Or a worship service will penetrate my hard heart and invade my busy mind, transporting me into the very presence of God. My spirit connects with his. "Come quickly," I'll whisper. "I want to see Jesus."

One day I will see him, and his reward will be with him. Not for anything I've attained but what he's attained for me.

Come quickly, Lord. Amen.

Digging Deeper

1. After a hard day, what types of rewards do you give yourself? A soak in a hot bath? A slice of cheesecake? How do you reward others? What prompts you to do so? What types of rewards do you think God has for his people?

2. Using a concordance, look up the word *reward*. What does the Bible say about God rewarding his people? To get started, see Genesis 15:1; Psalm 17:14; Proverbs 14:14; Isaiah 40:10; Colossians 3:24.

3. Ecclesiastes 3:11 tells us that God has put eternity in our hearts. What do you think that means? Read Romans 8:18-25 and 2 Corinthians 5:1-5. What do these passages say about the longings of our hearts?

4. Our reward isn't just future. Eternal life begins at the time of conversion. What rewards do we enjoy here on earth? Read the following passages and make a list of our present rewards: Jeremiah 31:3; Lamentations 3:22-23; Romans 5:1; 8:11,16-17,31; Galatians 5:1; Ephesians 1:4-9. What other rewards can you think of? Write a prayer to God thanking him for all his good and perfect gifts.

"If I find in myself desires nothing in this world can satisfy, the only logical explanation is that I was made for another world."

—C. S. LEWIS, *The Quotable Lewis*

About the Author

As a freelance writer since 1989, Nancy Kennedy has written several books, including *Prayers God Always Answers; Move Over, Victoria—I Know the Real Secret!; When He Doesn't Believe* (WaterBrook Press); and *Between Two Loves* (Zondervan, 2003). Her work has also appeared in *Christian Parenting Today, Today's Christian Woman, Marriage Partnership,* and many other publications.

Currently she's a feature writer, editor, and columnist for her local daily newspaper, the *Citrus County Chronicle.* Her religion-page features have won several First Place Excellence in Religion Writing awards from the Florida Press Club.

You can read her weekly column, "Grace Notes," as well as some of her articles that appear online, through her Web site at www.nancykennedy books.net.

To contact Nancy Kennedy, e-mail her through her Web site or write her in care of Seven Rivers Presbyterian Church, 4221 W. Gulf-to-Lake Hwy., Lecanto, FL 34461.